NESTS AND STRANGERS

NESTS AND STRANGERS

ON ASIAN AMERICAN WOMEN POETS

Edited with an Introduction by Timothy Yu

Afterword by Mg Roberts

KELSEY STREET PRESS

KELSEY STREET PRESS

2824 Kelsey Street, Berkeley, CA 94705

info@kelseyst.com www.kelseyst.com

Library of Congress Cataloging-in-Publication Data

Nests and strangers : on Asian American women poets /

edited with an introduction by Timothy Yu ; afterword by Mg Roberts.

pages cm

Includes bibliographical references.

ISBN 978-0-932716-81-1 (pbk. : alk. paper)

1. American poetry—Asian American authors—History and criticism.

2. American poetry—Women authors—History and criticism.

I. Yu, Timothy (Professor of literature) editor.

PS153.A84N46 2014

811.009'895—dc23

2014023622

Volume Editor: Timothy Yu

Copy Editor: Ramsay Bell Breslin

Production Editor: Mg Roberts

Designed by Quemadura

Printed on acid-free, recycled paper

in the United States of America

SPECULATIVE NOTES ON BHANU
KAPIL'S MONSTROUS/CYBORGIAN/
SCHIZOPHRENIC POETICS

DOROTHY WANG

78

NOTES TOWARD AN AFTERWORD

WHAT ENTRAILS

MG ROBERTS

92

CONTRIBUTORS

97

ACKNOWLEDGMENTS

99

PREFACE

Nests and Strangers: On Asian American Women Poets represents
Kelsey Street's first book of essays in the area of cultural studies. The
collection documents the intersection of four Kelsey Street Press au-
thors on the essayists' thinking, teaching, and on their own writing.
Each piece, including Timothy Yu's Introduction and Mg Roberts's
"Notes Toward an Afterword," contributes insight into the ways in
which poetry refuses limits set by cultural prejudices, political norms,
and the human body, opening up new possibilities for language
within the fluid architecture of shifting personal and collective iden-
tities. Now, in 2014, this anthology stands as a rare, unexpected event
—an answer to a publisher's wish to see its authors' works received,
used by others in their own thinking and writing, and passed on.
Nests and Strangers is such a pleasure and a fitting celebration of four
decades of small press writing and publishing.

PATRICIA DIENSTFREY

Co-founder with Rena Rosenwasser of Kelsey Street Press

NESTS AND STRANGERS

ON ASIAN AMERICAN

WOMEN POETS

The four writers whose work is discussed in these pages—Nellie Wong, Mei-mei Berssenbrugge, Myung Mi Kim, and Bhanu Kapil—represent the full range of Asian American poetry written since the 1970s. The Asian American political movement of that decade brought with it a flowering of Asian American literature, and poetry played a role in that renaissance that is still largely unacknowledged. Poetry was a fixture in activist journals such as *Gidra* and *Bridge* and featured prominently in movement anthologies like *Roots: An Asian American Reader*.

It's tempting to suppose that the poets most closely associated with the Asian American movement were those whose writing most frequently wore its politics on its sleeve. The poetry of Nellie Wong, as Merle Woo eloquently demonstrates in her essay for this collection, has always been closely tied to Wong's activist commitments. Her poems speak directly to her working-class experiences and to her socialist and feminist struggles. But Mei-mei Berssenbrugge, a poet more frequently discussed in terms of her use of abstraction and her collaborations with visual artists than her political commitments, was also a central fixture of the activist literary scene. Berssenbrugge's work appeared in movement anthologies, and as Sueyeun

Juliette Lee writes in her contribution to this collection, Berssenbrugge's association with the Basement Workshop, with its focus on community outreach and Asian American arts programming, was central to her own career and to that of other writers whom she mentored in her workshops.

Reading Wong and Berssenbrugge alongside each other, as we are invited to do here, quickly makes clear that there is no easy equivalence between political engagement and aesthetics. The ferment of the activist decade of the 1970s spawned a dizzying variety of aesthetic responses. Critic George Uba's distinction between the "activist" poetics of the 1970s and the "post-activist" poetry of the 1980s and 1990s, while useful as a generational marker, overlooks the aesthetic diversity of the poetry of the activist era.[1] Instead, we can see Wong and Berssenbrugge engaged in a conversation about the politics of Asian American poetic form, pursuing different modes that flow from the emergence of the category of Asian American identity.

The poetry of Myung Mi Kim and Bhanu Kapil extends this conversation. Both are of the "post-activist" era in that they began publishing in the 1990s, and their work reflects the critiques of identity politics and cultural nationalism characteristic of that decade. As Sarah Dowling discusses in her essay, Kim resists presenting a stable autobiographical subject who might tell a conventional Asian American story, while Kapil, in *Humanimal*, moves to seemingly remote subject matter, addressing the story of two girls raised by wolves in India. But as this collection shows, both engage the same intersection of politics, aesthetics, and history that Berssenbrugge and Wong do, from the scenes of language learning and migration in Kim's *Under Flag* to Kapil's meditations on colonialism and identity.

4

Despite the rich body of poetry by Asian Americans, the study of Asian American poetry remains a relatively unexplored field with the first book-length studies appearing only within the past few years. Remarkably enough, this book is the first collection of essays on Asian American women poets, and it thus offers a perspective that is long overdue.

Kelsey Street Press's championing of women poets and writers of color has given its publications an outsized impact in the realm of Asian American writing. Nellie Wong's *Dreams in Harrison Railroad Park* appeared in 1983, making it among the first full-length poetry collections by an Asian American woman. Kelsey Street has supported Mei-mei Berssenbrugge's work throughout her long career, publishing five of her books, beginning with *Sphericity* in 1993—often in unusual formats that accommodate Berssenbrugge's distinctively long lines and her collaborations with visual artists. Myung Mi Kim's debut collection, *Under Flag*, published by Kelsey Street in 1998, has become a widely taught text and contains Kim's most frequently discussed poems. Kelsey Street also published Bhanu Kapil's debut collection, *The Vertical Interrogation of Strangers*, in 2001—the first of two books by Kapil published by Kelsey Street—highlighting a unique and innovative new voice, one which represented the extension of Asian American poetry beyond East Asian American writers and into diasporic sensibilities.

Taken together, these books reveal poetry by Asian American women as a relentlessly *experimental* practice, in the broadest sense of that word: not a particular set of formal techniques, but a willingness to regard all elements of a poem—political, contextual, biographical, formal—as truly open. Wong's willingness to disrupt poetic

5

convention and decorum with direct statements of radical politics finds an echo in Kim's use of found material, critique of official discourses, and investigation of the roots of speech. Berssenbrugge's philosophical explorations of perception and personhood are extended in Kapil's work at the boundaries of identities and places— human/animal, intimate/stranger. Yet none takes the project of writing as an Asian American woman as fixed or determinate; indeed, all challenge the fixity of identity by engaging overlapping, cross-cutting identifications.

The four essays collected here take approaches as diverse as those taken by the Asian American poets who are their subjects. Sarah Dowling's essay on Myung Mi Kim adopts a new approach to Kim's widely discussed poetry by addressing an apparent paradox in Kim's work: Kim shares with many experimental writers a suspicion of a stable speaking subject, but her work nonetheless succeeds in plumbing personal and lyrical depths. Dowling highlights Kim's interest in the *other* voices—other languages, discourses, ideologies—that can circumscribe the space of subjectivity, becoming "so much louder" than the voice of the subject. Kim, Dowling argues, is just as interested in the way a subject may *not* come into being; Kim's poetry takes on the impossible, yet necessary, task of tracing the personhood of those whose personhood is denied: women, migrants, the colonized.

A retrospective on Nellie Wong's long career as poet and activist is offered by her longtime friend and comrade Merle Woo, whose essay, like Wong's work itself, blends poetics, biography, and radical political commitment. Woo's wide-ranging study begins with Wong's childhood in Oakland, California, follows her development into a radical feminist and socialist, and outlines her close relationships with the working-class and Asian American communities for whom she struggles and speaks. Woo's essay is less an appreciation of Wong's work than a complement to it; beginning with a powerful evocation of the "urgent present" within which we live, Woo's reading of Wong is an engaged criticism that argues passionately for the deep link between poetry and political struggle.

Sueyeun Juliette Lee also argues for the link between poetry and politics in the work of a very different writer, Mei-mei Berssenbrugge. Berssenbrugge's work has often been approached from a phenomenological perspective that emphasizes her interest in perception and the body. While acknowledging the importance of such readings, Lee also seeks to restore historical and political context to Berssenbrugge's work. Lee's focus is on Berssenbrugge's rarely-discussed involvement with the Basement Workshop, a pioneering Asian American arts organization based in New York, and on Berssenbrugge's long association with the physical spaces of New York and New Mexico. Lee gives us a deeply enriched sense of the communities that shape Berssenbrugge's work, grounding her aesthetic experiments in lived experience and in Asian American history.

Among the four contributors, Dorothy Wang experiments most boldly with the essay form. Wang responds to Bhanu Kapil's innovative prose poetry by breaking up the critical voice of her essay, offering lists, collaged texts, and map-like catalogs of the locations across which Kapil's writing moves. Wang's central subject is the role of the "I" in Kapil's work, which, as in Kim's and Berssenbrugge's, is often unstable or under erasure, yet insistently present for all that. Wang intriguingly triangulates Kapil's "I" in relation to other schools of poetry, from the New York School to Flarf to Conceptualism. And as with the other poets under discussion in this volume, Wang finds that it is the category of the Asian American woman that disrupts established categories, providing a site for the critique of discourses of race, gender, and nation.

Taken together, these four essays make a forceful case for the centrality of Asian American women poets to contemporary literary and political discourse. The work of Wong, Berssenbrugge, Kim, and Kapil can be read as an ongoing inquiry into the conditions of subjectivity. Who gets to speak and how? How can personhood emerge from the welter of contemporary discourse, particularly when that discourse continues to be shaped by racism, sexism, and colonialism? By unearthing the contexts of Asian American poetry by women, the essays in this collection suggest that Asian American women poets offer distinctive interventions into the forces that shape our everyday lives, demonstrating the potentially transformative power of a poetry that negotiates the boundaries of race and gender.

TIMOTHY YU

NOTE

1. George Uba, "Versions of Identity in Post-Activist Asian American Poetry," in *Reading the Literatures of Asian America*, eds. Shirley Geok-lin Lim and Amy Ling (Philadelphia: Temple Univ. Press, 1992).

INTERPOLATION, COHERENCE, HISTORY

THE WORKS OF MYUNG MI KIM

SARAH DOWLING

In a recent conversation between the poets Myung Mi Kim and Divya Victor, Kim describes her use of quoted material without reference to appropriation, assemblage, citation, or other critical terms that call attention to the author's curatorial hand: "there is no decision here to include material or matter. It simply *couldn't* be avoided" (Kim's emphasis).[1] For Kim, agency seems to lie not with the poet, but with the text itself: "somehow, [the text] suddenly multiplies the terms of something you were thinking about, or it makes the conversation in your head become so much louder." Perhaps it is not so shocking to imagine the texts one encounters in the world as representative of a "conversation in your head." But what attracts me to Kim's comments on her process is her description of the "loudness" of this conversation: although it happens internally, "in your head," Kim implies that these silent texts really do have volume, even force. Rather than asking us to imagine the labor of the poet as an active process of ranging among, and choosing between, cultural texts, Kim explains that these loud texts "found *me*." In this process, foreign elements are interpolated into the text, corrupting it. These interpolated texts in turn interpellate the poet. They discover her, and the nature of her subjectivity is constituted through their intrusive loudness.

Much as Kim's description of her reliance upon material "that can be identified as 'another'" emphasizes her distinction from other appropriation-based poetries, her incorporation of other languages sets her apart from other avant-garde writers who have made multilingualism a cornerstone of their experiments in poetry.[2] Rather than the modernist impulse to shore up the fragments and reconstitute the mind of Europe, when Kim draws in material in other languages, she avoids the acquisitive range of her modernist precursors, as well as their insistence on "mak[ing] it new."[3] Instead of the abstract cultural ambitions of Pound's or Eliot's appropriative, multilingual epics, the material that can be identified as "another" language in Kim's poetry pushes back against widely-held assumptions that experimental poetry must make a radical break with the past. In her work, multilingualism and appropriation draw the past closer. As Joseph Jonghyun Jeon has argued, encounters with other languages form the essential texture of this poetry's sonic richness: some of the most ubiquitous sounds in Kim's poetry are the ones considered most difficult for native speakers of Korean to form in English.[4] Through its difficult multilingual sounds, Kim's work offers a "notat[ion]" of the "provisional location" of the present in relation to the archive of the past.[5] Her poems "counter the potential totalizing power of language that serves the prevailing systems and demands of coherence" by "measur[ing]" the "cathexis of the living instant to the acuteness of history" (110, 111).

In this respect, Kim's work presents an apparent paradox: in drawing upon personal archives of experience and emotion, she builds a rich sediment of lyric affects, such as loss and yearning. But she neither attaches nor attributes these affects to a conventional subject; instead, in reading her poems we hear that external conversation of quoted materials and other languages becoming "so much louder." Her poems carefully trace an absent center: there is no specific figure in the poems who hears this loudness or speaks these languages, or whom we might say is feeling the feelings provoked by the invasive external materials. In this way, Kim pursues a philosophical problem that she calls the "feminization of the problem of lived time" (108): how to write about the lives of subjects who have been "feminiz[ed]" or reduced; how to describe the ways in which one becomes—or, more importantly, *does not become*—a subject over time. Through the combination of interpolated texts and the sonic and affective density of the lyric, Kim represents those denied subjectivity—the status of the subject of legal rights, the socially legible person, or the expressive subject of poetry. Her works consider the ways in which personhood is delineated and limited, routinely denied.

Combining English and Korean, official document and private memory, Kim's poems frame the personal past as a kind of archive, not the continuous history of a unified self, but a collection of ephemera—memories, photographs, facts, letters. This archive records the ways in which the authorial self is found out by, or is unable to avoid, the forces and discourses that seek her out, in order to quantify, describe, and minimize her. Although Kim, like many other experimental poets, turns away from the depiction of an expressive speaking subject, her texts focus very closely on what is personal, specific, and contingent: her books frequently refer to painful episodes from her childhood and throughout her life. By colliding personal memory with official power, Kim provides a record of "the terms under which" one becomes, or does not become, a subject—legally, socially, or in poetry. Her poetry holds open the possibility of connection or coalition among these "feminiz[ed]" figures.

INTERPOLATION

In contemporary experimental poetics, the lyric is frequently criticized for being overly subjective and naively reliant upon experience and personal testimony. Even as many contemporary writers regard the field in which they are writing as beyond the lyric, the branding of certain texts—especially texts by women of color—as lyric is both persistent and ubiquitous.[6] Given the widespread criticism of lyric poetry, Kim's description of her poems as lyric seems especially notable. However, when Kim's references to personal history and her work's sonic density are viewed alongside her prodigious use of interpolation, the stakes of her reference to the lyric tradition change dramatically. In Kim's work, interpolation is closely linked to its homonym interpellation, which literary studies of the past few decades have borrowed from the Marxist philosopher Louis Althusser, as a term encompassing the way that ideology, embodied by social and political institutions, constitutes subjects' identities by "hailing" us in various social interactions. We learn to recognize ourselves in the roles of daughter, immigrant, poet, and so on; and it is only through these roles that we come to believe that we are autonomous individual agents.

The intertwining of interpolation and interpellation is especially apparent in "Into Such Assembly," one of the most powerful poems in *Under Flag* and a critical favorite.[7] The first section of the three-part poem begins:

> Can you read and write English? Yes _____. No _____.
> Write down the following sentences in English as I dictate them.
>   There is a dog in the road.
>   It is raining.
> Do you renounce allegiance to any other country but this?
> Now tell me, who is the president of the United States?
> You will all stand now. Raise your right hands. (29)

This stanza seems to quote from an English-language instructor and from a naturalization ceremony; the two quoted texts interpolate each other, corrupting one another until citizenship and linguistic facility almost appear coterminous. Moreover, they interpolate the poem fully—at this early point they *are* the poem in its entirety. The quoted passages also interpellate the addressee, the "you" of the poem we are invited to assume is the poet, as a would-be American, an immigrant desirous of citizenship. The final line of the first stanza even suggests that citizenship status is about to be conferred upon the addressee: "You will all stand now. Raise your right hands." Momentarily, we imagine, she and her citizenship class will attain their new status.

At the close of the first section of "Into Such Assembly," Kim asks, "Who is mother tongue, who is father country?" (Ibid.) As the second poem in the sequence makes clear, even if the speaker/addressee is able to achieve equality, legally and formally, through citizenship, her status is compromised by harsh social realities. Rather than being welcomed into the national family of "mother tongue" and "father country," the speaker/addressee is once again overwhelmed by intruding voices. The officialese used in the first poem in the sequence disappears in the second, which is interpolated instead by casual, everyday voices whose interpellations of the speaker are arguably more devastating:

2.

Do they have trees in Korea? Do the children eat out of garbage cans?

We had a dalmation
We rode the train on weekends from Seoul to So-Sah where we grew grapes

We ate on the patio surrounded by dahlias

Over there, ass is cheap—those girls live to make you happy

Over there, we had a slateblue house with a flat roof where I made many snowmen, over there

No, "th", "th", put your tongue against the roof of your mouth, lean slightly against the back of the top teeth, then bring your bottom teeth up to barely touch your tongue and breathe out, and you should feel the tongue vibrating, "th", "th", look in the mirror, that's better

And with distance traveled, as part of it

How often when it rains here does it rain there?

One gives over to a language and then

What was given, given over? (30)

This section turns upon its contrast between the speaker's fond memories of Korea and the interpolated text, quoted material running the gamut from ignorant curiosity to Orientalist sexual fantasies, to quasi-therapeutic corrections. In the interstices between the speaker's memories of her dog, pleasant journeys, beautiful flowers, her home and her snowmen, external voices intrude, stopping up her voice, sometimes literally, with intense and detailed interventions: "No, 'th', 'th.'" These interpolated texts hail the speaker as a foreigner, garbage-eating, sexually eager-to-please, and unable to truly speak—not fully or properly a person. In the final lines, when the speaker asks, "What was given, given over" in "giv[ing] over to a language," answers to her question hover silently in the reader's mind: her memories, her ability to articulate them without hindrance, and her personhood seem to have been "given over" in the transition to English.

Kim has continued to pursue these dynamics in her subsequent books. In *Commons*, she attends to small bits of sound, "random, skittish stutterings," that she imagines as "potential sounds in Korean or, for that matter, in any number of languages (Middle English, Latin, French) that constitute English"[8] These incipient or "potential sounds" frequently transition into actual words, either in Korean or

in English. This linguistic multiplicity, which Kim values for its con-
notations of possibility, receives harsh treatment when other voices
intrude and pass judgment upon it. For example, in the following sec-
tion of the poem "Lamenta," it is clear that even explicit connections
between Korean and English words cannot redeem the "random,
skittish stutterings" or the words in Korean.[9] Instead, they are con-
sidered only as "noise":

506

a̲p̲
ac

Pock

ji-wuat-dah   erased

jil-eu-dah   shouted

Regarded among penury

Numb pie mum pie

jip-sae-gi ji-pah-raeng-e   :   show here

Look at that noise!

Numb pie mum pie (52)

The progression of this poem from the sounds "ap" and "ac" into words in Korean and English positions these sounds as fragments of potential meaning. Rather than being valued for their potential, however, these "stutterings" are instead "[r]egarded among penury," viewed in the context of lack. They are "Numb" sounds with no referent. It is clear that the Korean phrases share something with the English ones ("Regarded" and "Look" are semantically linked to *"jip-sae-gi ji-pah-raeng-e,"* translated as "show here"), but the possibility of pursuing that connection is foreclosed. When the words and sounds that are not in English are dismissed as "that noise" and are mimicked in the repeated phrase, "Numb pie mum pie," it is clear that they are considered not in terms of their actual or potential meaning, but only in terms of their "penury," their failure to mean in English.

Especially when viewed alongside "Into Such Assembly," the attributions of meaninglessness in "Lamenta" reveal that language is one of the grounds upon which personhood is denied. Failure to conform linguistically leaves one "among penury," as mere "noise." Kim's sentence fragments are striking for their conspicuous lack of either a subject or an object: lines such as *"ji-wuat-dah* erased" [sic] and "Regarded among penury" are suggestive of actions, but not of who performs them, or upon whom. Sourceless and directionless, they seem to come from a human body, since they fall under the heading of "pock," but after all, a pock is not so much a part of a body as the absence of one of its parts, a place where a piece of that body has been scratched away or consumed by infection. More violently, "pock" is also "an abrupt and percussive sound," such as "a bullet striking a wall,"[10] and thus the actions listed below it perhaps refer to the fren-

17

zied confusion that follows such a noise. Ultimately, these actions and sounds remain meaningless; while it is possible to project various scenarios from their combination, or to imagine the bodies that perform them or the bodies upon whom they are performed, the negative judgment against them that unifies the poem's sound is most clear in the phrase, "Look at that noise!

Kim's frequent citation of these negative judgments, the attribution of meaninglessness to the figures who appear briefly or partially in her poems, has much to do with the historical contexts referenced in her poetry. In the wake of the Immigration and Nationality Act of 1965, immigration to the United States doubled between 1965 and 1970, and then doubled again between 1970 and 1990, with the greatest increases coming from Asia and South and Central America. Mae M. Ngai, studying the period from 1924–1965, just prior to Kim's immigration and to the period that her poems in *Under Flag* consider, argues that sharp restrictions on immigration in the early-to mid-twentieth century "produced the illegal alien as a *new legal and political subject,* whose inclusion within the nation was simultaneously a social reality and a legal impossibility—a subject barred from citizenship and without rights."[11]

Kim's poems depict the aftereffects of this legal change, the new reality inaugurated by the rapid and dramatic increase of Asian immigration to the US. Kim does not suggest that the figures she depicts are without legal rights; instead, she demonstrates that inclusion is at once legal reality and a social impossibility. The new immigrants interrogated about their homelands could be American citizens, and subjects of legal rights may well utter the evocative linguistic fragments mocked for their penurious failure to mean. But what is the meaning of those rights when the subject to whom they are attached is socially understood as meaningless, or can scarcely be perceived as a subject at all?

COHERENCE

In her introduction to Myung Mi Kim's reading at the Kelly Writers House at the University of Pennsylvania on March 14th, 2007, Josephine Nock-Hee Park explains that Kim's work is characterized by a foundational incoherence: the division of Korea along the 38th parallel.[12] While Ezra Pound lamented that he could not make the fragments in his poetry cohere, Kim instructs herself to "counter the potential totalizing power of language that serves the prevailing systems and demands of coherence."[13] Poems such as "Demarcation" in *Under Flag* and "Thirty and Five Books" in *Dura* (Nightboat Books, 2008) reveal the extent and purpose of Kim's refusal of coherence. They offer narratives of immigrant experience, but layer multiple histories together, refusing to present a clear trajectory of arrival and assimilation, instead creating analogies and connections across different historical experiences. These poems focus as much on American actions in Korea as on Korean actions in America. They describe historical events that fall within the span of the poet's life, but place this history in dialogue with other histories of colonialism, drawing upon geographically and temporally distant events. If the "demands of coherence" would prevent these unexpected connections from being drawn, Kim's refusal of coherence allows tenuous and unexpected links to emerge.

"Demarcation" serves as an early example of Kim's critique of coherence. The poem describes disjunctions between the natural world and its representation in language, focusing on new political realities inaugurated by the tracing of fresh borders: "No trace on earth of what is said // No way to put palm up against it."[14] Its final lines read:

> As a compass locates relocates and cuts fresh figures
> As silence to mate(d) world
>
> Not founded by mother or father
> Spun into coherence (cohere)
>
> Cohere who can say (38)

The "compass locates relocates" the geographic borders of the country, cutting the "fresh figures" of North and South Korea, which are "not founded by mother or father." Instead, as Park suggests, these two countries are "spun into coherence" through repetitive insistence: "cohere who can say." Language makes it so. The "fresh figures" that language cuts are not only national, however. We have seen the play of interpolation and interpellation that cuts patterns for fresh new kinds of figures like the embattled speaker/addressee of "Into Such Assembly." But in "Demarcation" Kim suggests that figures like her may also be freshly cut, in the sense of wounding: as the compass locates and relocates, it finds and produces new victims. "Demarcation," then, focuses on failures of language: "As the infant face is absence onto which we say / It is like — it is like —" (38). The statement is never finished, and the speaker's voice wavers in silence, refusing to collude in the cutting by offering a simplistic, coherent statement to satisfy the child. If the word "demarcation" typically suggests clarity, this poem emphasizes the "absence" of the "infant face" and the inability to provide good answers.

Kim's critique of coherence continues across her oeuvre: in *Dura*, the poem "Thirty and Five Books" quotes from *Sa-I-Gu*, a multilingual documentary film presenting Korean American women's perspectives on the April 1992 unrest in Los Angeles.[15] One of the film's central narratives focuses on the only Korean American fatality, Edward Song Lee, an eighteen-year-old boy shot by a fellow Korean American who mistook him for a looter. Kim incorporates the testimony of Jung Hui Lee, the victim's mother, interspersing her lines with other quoted material, particularly Aristotle's *On the Heavens*.[16] Lee's testimony emphasizes her confusion in the wake of her son's killing. Kim's combination of this testimony with Aristotle's remarks on the movement of fire approximates the terrifying confusion felt during the riots in Los Angeles:

> Extinguished   spreading
>
>   He was wearing a white T-shirt and jeans
>
> Beat fresh the burning
>
>   The boy in the newspaper wore a dark shirt
>
> Flakes of fire ripen fire
>
>   It could not be my son
>
> Agate of insistence
>
>   Contents of the boy's pocket — a dime and a pen
>
> Percussive
>
>   In the *LA Times* the picture was in color
>
> Body moving in circle be fire
>
>   What looked black in Korean newspaper was
>
>   my son's blood
>
> Body moving in circle be fire
>
> If fire be the body carried round[17]

The indented lines in this passage represent Lee's testimony in the film, which Kim appears to offer in her own translation. (There are slight differences between the subtitles and Kim's quotations.) Josephine Nock-Hee Park reads this episode as a "literalization of [Theresa Hak Kyung] Cha's conflation of blood and ink" in *Dictée*, with the crucial difference that Lee's blood "does not have an expressive function; it is only the result of violence."[18] Indeed, Kim emphasizes the anti-expressive function of blood and ink both: black ink and colored ink present contradictory evidence, alternately denying and confirming Lee's worst fears for her son. Like the motion of fire, the facts swirl, jump, and mutate; but unlike Aristotle's descriptions of rational and perfect motion in the heavens, in the historical context Kim describes, there is no reason or perfection, only the upward and downward gusts of destructive flames.

Early in *Sa-I-Gu*, one of the first women to offer testimony, Young Soon Han, explains that she's "angry at everybody, or on the contrary I'm angry at myself, because I don't know to whom, to where I should be angry . . . I'm totally confused."[19] These remarks are useful in reading Kim's borrowings from the documentary: rather than a simplistic catalogue of blame or even a lament, Kim traces connections between historical events so as to draw the communities involved in the violence in Los Angeles closer together: "Torch and fire. Translate: 38th parallel. Translate: / the first shipload of African slaves was landed at Jamestown" (62). Both Korean Americans and African Americans become "players in the field of manipulation. // For such a purpose fit who least have" (63).

Although Lee's words are among the most haunting and poignant lyric moments in *Dura*'s transnational epic, they are strikingly disembodied: upon first reading, it is impossible to know who is speaking.[20] By drawing in Lee's words, Kim reveals a conversation in the process of becoming so much louder, but she refuses to present simplistic and predictable positions for the interlocutors. Instead, Kim strips back identifying characteristics and focuses on the commonalities of "torch and fire": what draws the participants in the conversation together is their shared vulnerability to being burned by those who most "have." It is only through Kim's principled refusal of coherence that these connections become apparent.

HISTORY

In her introduction to its 2008 reissue, Juliana Spahr argues that a "major assumption" of *Dura* is that "identity and subjectivity are formed within a net of cultures, not just one" (x). *Dura*, Spahr contends, is self-conscious about "be[ing] told in language, a thing that one must share with others in a particularly complicated way that is all tied up ... with culture and nation" (x). Although Spahr emphasizes Kim's "net of cultures" and the questions of language and nation, she also describes *Dura* as "an immigrant's story, one full of stuttering language," and cites Kim's own description of the project as a "kind of strange autobiography," one "built out of fragments" that avoid both the "I" and "the sentence's finality" (x). Spahr's introduction suggests the contours of the critical work on Kim's oeuvre: critics have frequently discussed her work's debt to the lyric tradition, considering it within the framework of an immigrant poetics, while

23

also calling attention to the use of unconventional, experimental forms in its "strange autobiography." What is "strange" about this autobiography, I think, is that it generally avoids individualizing its autobiographical subject. Rather than a story of development over time, Kim focuses on what happens to figures who are denied developmental narratives, figures who are tasked with simply enduring.

One of the poems in *Penury*, "fell (for six multilingual voices)," is a choral piece that enacts and expands the coalitions imagined in *Dura*.[21] Kim draws on dramatic conventions for rendering dialogue in order to create the sense that something or someone is minimized or missing. Most of the lines in "fell" begin with two punctuation marks, which seem at once to indicate and erase the identity of the speaker:

> : | Measure streets by the number of uniforms
>
> : | It's the pitch of the cry that carries
>
> : | Hunger noise thirst noise fear noise
>
> : | Inside acts conducted outside
>
> : | Decades of continuous drought
>
> : | Weapon and deed (51)

The blankness to the left of the colon beginning each line suggests a space for a name, as though the identity of the speaker has been eliminated from the poem. The short, spare lines that follow provide no further clues as to who is speaking. Having attended and participated in a performance of this piece, I also see the blank space to the left of the colon as a kind of invitation: anyone might speak these lines. Kim's specification that "fell" is "for six multilingual voices" makes clear that speakers' accents (or even translations) would become part of the poem's texture and meaning in each performance, that these would lend distinctive nuances and meanings to the "number of uniforms," "decades of continuous drought," and "weapon[s] and deed[s]" named in the text. The poem is open to a broad variety of speakers and works to create a common experience across their differences. However, in order to create this commonality, Kim reduces their speech to the barest elements. By avoiding specific, individualized tales, the speakers in "fell" reveal the commonalities of what has befallen them.

Nevertheless, Kim's work is recognizably autobiographical in its tendency to refer to and represent episodes and moments in the poet's personal history. But because she focuses on hidden, ghostly subjects whose status as subjects (legal and poetic) is compromised by the preponderance of the social and its becoming "so much louder," her use of autobiographical detail differs significantly from both the lyric model of confession and the evacuation of subjectivity that has long characterized experimental poetics. Instead, Kim's projects are characterized by cross-temporal cleaving: rather than the sweep of the national epic, she examines history on the scales of the sentimental and the quotidian. Kim is particularly concerned with the reduction—the feminization, as she calls it—of temporality. In her work, there is no clear subject reflecting back on the past, nor is there a clear subject in the past upon whom one might reflect. And yet, there is much reflection on the past; through this cross-temporal cleaving, Kim considers the problem of how one becomes, or is prevented from becoming, a subject over time. Denied the legibility and coherence of a future-oriented narrative, Kim's works instead explore the potential of the past, and of non-developmental forms.

The poem "Thirty and Five Books" in *Dura* provides a beautiful example of this "strange autobiography," in which vulnerability and pathos receive pride of place. Not too long after the passage in which Kim quotes Lee's mother's heartbreaking testimony, she includes a chronologically ordered list of life events that seem to be her own. However, as much as Kim minimizes the characteristics that might identify Lee, this section is also radically depersonalized and extremely spare:

:   :

6.1   How expressed

6.4   There must have been ten or more tadpoles in the jar

7.2   Number, form, proportion, situation

8.5   Fried meat dumplings and sweet rice cakes

9.8   One of the first words understood in English: stupid

10.9   Diamondback on Oklahoma red dirt

11.4   A lambswool coat for straight A's

12.6   This immediate problem of reporting

14.8   Lightning struck the roof father spinning on ice
        and killed which happened in what order

16.9   Certainty, possibility, impossibility

17.8   Models of reality compared with experience

18.1   Time whose points are events

:   :

20.6   Only one   there are none

21.0   Love postulates dinnerware in the cupboard

22.11   Brackets, their importance

25.9   Clues to pressure and thaw

27.7   The name of that town is

28.3   A million marching in the streets

29.1   The barn the shed the trough the pasture

30.2   Four roads meeting precisely at a grid

32.10   Given birth 5:05AM

33.0   The subject is a proposition

34.0   Impulse of vocal air

35.0   If seventy is the sum of our years[22]

The numbers on the left-hand side of this poem refer to years and
months of Kim's life, and the corresponding lines to particular
events: her father's death, the birth of her son, and so on. Of course,
some of the items included within this list are not events but vivid
images: "tadpoles in the jar," "Diamondback on Oklahoma red dirt,"
or "Four roads meeting precisely at a grid." Others describe situa-

tions: "This immediate problem of reporting," or "Love postulates dinnerware in the cupboard." The balance is made up of realizations: the meaning of the word "stupid," "Models of reality compared with experience," "The subject is a proposition," or "If seventy is the sum of our years." Many of the items in this list conform to the recognizable categories of what Jack Halberstam has called the "paradigmatic markers of life experience," the events that make a life recognizable as such. But the radically spare character of the list means that it is only the numerical sequence of the left-hand column that directly evokes a life and brings these diverse fragments and images together.[23] The spaces between the colons that seem to hold the place of titles are left blank; nothing at all appears in the spot where someone's name might have been.

The linearity of Kim's list, its references to normative life events, and its depiction of significant realizations resonate with (auto)biographical forms. And yet, the use of the list and the numerical notation of the passing of life place this depiction at a great distance from more normative forms of life writing. In particular, the final line of the poem, "If seventy is the sum of our years," is striking: if indeed this is true, then the thirty-five sections in Kim's poem record exactly half a life, stopping at its mid-point and thereby departing significantly from more standard autobiography. In the excerpt from "Thirty and Five Books" that I have quoted, only one brief line for each year or event is included, and there is no development from "How expressed" to "If seventy is the sum of our years," from age six to thirty-five.

In "Pollen Fossil Record," Kim describes her work as a consideration of temporality. If "becoming a historical subject" (108) is a process that unfolds over time, she asks, how does this process take place for "remote, castigated" subjects such as the impoverished or the feminized (108)? This description illuminates the formal strangeness of "Thirty and Five Books": if Kim's project is to explore "feminiz[ed]" subjects and their temporalities, then indeed the reduction of the "Books" in the title to extremely brief and spare poetic lines fits perfectly. Furthermore, the title's description of the poem is instructive: the first six of the "Thirty and Five Books" have been lost, and of the remaining twenty-nine, only one line from each appears. Rather than the expanse, the narrative progression, or the ontological certainty of autobiography, the "feminiz[ed]" subject, the "remote, castigated" subject, appears only as "a proposition." In other words, in spite of the normative life events that appear on Kim's list, the status of the figure to whom the list of events refers is not certain; her subjectivity is put forth as a possibility, not guaranteed.

This "chronicling lived time: registering the continuum of history" (109) pulls in two directions: on the one hand is history, an official timeline; on the other is the "lived," a feminized time that is real and unavoidable, but unstructured, merely endured. Nostalgic "chronicling" and "registering" presuppose a historical span, but the contention that "time" is only "lived" suggests that there is no development across it; indeed, given the content of Kim's work, perhaps it would be more accurate to say that time is not just "lived" but lived *through*; rather than progress, Kim's poems deal with duration and survival. In Kim's work, the passage of time is non-developmental and is explored through a "kind of strange," radically depersonalized autobiography, in which it is only the numerical notation of time's passing that reveals the ongoing, but almost invisible, presence of a lyric subject, or of multiple lyric subjects.

CONVERSATION

In this essay, I have examined several of Kim's books—*Under Flag*, *Dura*, *Commons*, and *Penury*—tracing the contours of the conversations within and between them, and the ways these texts record broader cultural conversations that seem to be constantly becoming "so much louder." Focusing on Kim's treatment of her appropriated or interpolated texts and these texts' treatment of her, I show how Kim explores and represents the social meaninglessness of those who are left on the sidelines, who are refused welcome into the family of "mother tongue" and "father country." Kim's careful and principled refusal of large-scale "systems of coherence" enables her to form more tenuous and difficult connections, which are realized as coalition in the vocal overlapping of "fell." If Kim begins from the unique marginalizations experienced by immigrants very much like herself, her poetry refuses to endow these figures with the fullness of poetic subjectivity or autobiographical development. It is only by keeping them "feminized," "remote," and "castigated" that she makes a space to explore the problem of duration encountered by the figures who enter her poetry: how will they go on? How will the poem give form to their doing and having done so?

In her interview with Divya Victor, Kim explains that she is "not necessarily working in the experimental tradition, or building on a genealogy of an experimental convention as it exists." Rather than "taking a *departure* from something that exists," she argues, her project is to "mak[e] it for the first time":

> How can I find a way to indicate the actual experience when that experience doesn't exist? There are no models, no modes, no form, no linguistic registers that are available. In a sense, you have to rework the entire continuum of language, form, prosody, whatever you're drawn to as a poet ... You have to *literally* make it. Hand by hand, finger by finger, foot by foot. You have to make something that allows you, however uncomfortably or comfortably, to work that space — mentally, emotionally, historically, and culturally. Because nothing exists for how you are coming to your own *condition*.
>
> [Kim's emphasis]

Kim's remarks here are especially instructive. It is easy to approach a poetic text with preconceptions about which traditions it fits into and how it fits into them, or about how the author's gender or ethnic background shapes her work. But Kim's comments remind us to read with fresh eyes, attentive to the particularities of every poem. Rather than assuming that an experimental text will not represent a lyric subject, rather than assuming that an experimental text will break with the past, rather than assuming that a text's incoherence has only to do with the materiality of language, we must instead attend to the poem's grappling with "how you are coming to your own *condition*."

Rather than making it new, this is a poetics of making it—of endurance, duration, lasting, and at times even of succeeding. This is a poetics investigating the need to make it, a poetics that inquires into the historical conditions that would prevent one from having made it already. Kim's work asks us to orient ourselves toward all those who were making it (and not making it) in the past, who are making it (and are not making it) right now. And perhaps in attending to those shared, precarious conditions, we might think about our own ability to extend a hand, and to make with them, to work on a more stable and humane future.

NOTES

1. Divya Victor and Myung Mi Kim, "Eight Discourses Between Myung Mi Kim and Divya Victor," *Jacket2*, March 5, 2011, https://jacket2.org/interviews/eight-discourses-between-myung-mi-kim-and-divya-victor.

2. Ibid.

3. "[M]aking it new" references the title of Ezra Pound's *Make It New* (New Haven: Yale Univ. Press, 1935).

4. Joseph Jonghyun Jeon, *Racial Things, Racial Forms: Objecthood in Avant-Garde Asian American Poetry* (Iowa City: Univ. of Iowa Press, 2012).

5. Myung Mi Kim, "Pollen Fossil Record," *Commons* (Berkeley: Univ. of California Press, 2002), 105–111.

6. For an excellent synopsis of these debates as they pertain to Asian Americans, see Timothy Yu, "Form and Identity in Language Poetry and Asian American Poetry," *Contemporary Literature* 41.3 (2000), 422–461.

7. Myung Mi Kim, "Into Such Assembly," *Under Flag* (Berkeley: Kelsey Street Press, 1991), 29–31.

8. Kim, *Commons*, 109.

9. Ibid.

10. *Oxford English Dictionary*, 2nd. ed., s.v., "pock"

11. Mae Ngai, *Impossible Subjects: Illegal Aliens and the Making of Modern America* (Princeton: Princeton Univ. Press, 2005), 4.

12. See also Josephine Nock-Hee Park, "'Composed of Many Lengths of Bone': Myung Mi Kim's Reimagination of Image and Epic" in *Transnational Asian American Literature: Sites and Transits*, eds. Shirley Geok-lin Lim, John Blair Gamber, Stephen Hong Sohn, and Gina Valentino (Philadelphia: Temple Univ. Press, 2006), 235–256.

13. Kim, "Pollen Fossil Record," *Commons*, 110.

14. Kim, "Demarcation," *Under Flag*, 37.

15. Dai Sil Kim-Gibson, Christine Choy, and Elaine Kim, *Sa-I-Gu: From Korean Women's Perspectives* (San Francisco: Cross-Current Media, 1993).

16. See W. K. C. Guthrie's translation in *Readings in Ancient Greek Philosophy: from Thales to Aristotle*, 4th Edition, eds. S. Marc Cohen, Patricia Curd, and C. D. C. Reeve (Indianapolis: Hackett Publishing Company, 2011), 777–784.

17. Myung Mi Kim, "Thirty and Five Books," *Dura* (New York: Nightboat Books, 2008), 58–59. Reprinted with permission of Nightboat Books.

18. Josephine Nock-Hee Park, *Apparitions of Asia: Modernist Form and Asian American Poetics* (Oxford: Oxford Univ. Press, 2008), 152.

19. *Sa-I-Gu*, Dir. Dai Sil Kim-Gibson and Christine Choy (1993), 5:13–5:28.

20. I was directed to watching *Sa-I-Gu* after reading Xiaojing Zhou's "'What Story What Story What Sound': The Nomadic Poetics of Myung Mi Kim's *Dura*," *College Literature* 34.4 (2007), 63–91.

21. Myung Mi Kim, "fell (for six multilingual voices)," *Penury* (Richmond: Omnidawn, 2009), 49–59.

22. Myung Mi Kim, "Thirty and Five Books," *Dura* (New York: Nightboat Books, 2008), 73–74. Reprinted with permission of Nightboat Books.

23. Judith Halberstam, *In a Queer Time and Place: Transgender Bodies, Subcultural Lives* (New York: New York Univ. Press, 2005), 2.

FEMINISM, LOVE,

AND REVOLUTION

THE POETIC VISION OF NELLIE WONG

MERLE WOO

In an interview on *PBS NewsHour* (9/18/2013), Edwidge Danticat, author of the recently published *Claire of the Sea Light*, said, "All writers, we reach back, but we also reach forward. And there is acknowledgement of the present; and for Haiti, it is an *urgent* present." We are indeed living in an *urgent* present. The entire globe is in an upheaval: wars, poverty, starvation, climate change leading to natural disasters. We are in dire need of a hopeful but realistic literature that offers solutions, not in an idealistic or "wishful thinking" way, but in a rational, concrete way. In the depths of decadent capitalism, with the world in tatters, we look to the powerful intuition of the Revolutionary Artist—an artist like Nellie Wong, with her audacity and independence (from traditional values)—to offer a social analysis with answers. She is not above us but definitely with us, the common Asian American woman, at one with the fate of mankind, in the difficult, tragic, *urgent* present, with wealth and power at one pole, misery and destitution on the other.

This essay is an attempt to portray Nellie Wong's poetry and writings as truly revolutionary art, which inspires and is hopeful, because it is based in concrete reality. Born in Oakland in 1934, Ms. Wong is our chronicler of a very specific history, located in a particular place and time: her story of her family, of Ma and *Bah Bah* and seven siblings growing up and working at the Great China Restaurant in Oakland's Chinatown; then working as a secretary in the San Francisco Bay Area for over thirty-five years. With another family (now revolutionary feminist comrades), she became a political activist in Radical Women, a "trailblazing socialist feminist organization,"[1] and served for sixteen years (1990–2006) as the Bay Area Organizer of the Freedom Socialist Party.

For most of her life, Wong has shown what it's like to be on the front lines every day, whether at work as a secretary whose thirst for knowledge threatened her bosses, or on the streets—marching with thousands, demanding justice—fighting for women's rights; studying poetry; immersing herself in family, comrades, community; writing our stories, saving our lives. With boundless love for her people, Nellie is, at the same time, refreshingly atheist. Collective humanity is her *deity*. The union of her socialist feminist ideology and active participation in the world informs her poetic consciousness, making possible a great art so necessary in these times. Her working-class sensibility captures the humility of the common people through direct contact with the life of her class, while her poetry gives us hope and inspiration through its expressions of beauty in the world found right outside our front doors: "Knowing the real history of people of color, immigrants, and workers that was denied me when I was young has deepened my commitment to write with love and revolutionary optimism . . . The ordinary, daily struggles of working women like those of the Lee Mah factory in my poem "Revolutionary Love" continue to remind me that there's work to be done. And through that, joy."[2]

In *Breakfast Lunch Dinner*, Wong's poetry reaches its highest form: radical realism. With sophisticated rhythms and rhymes and revolutionary detail, the poet advocates for the consolidation of workers in their struggle against their bosses. Solidarity with family, community, co-workers, union brothers and sisters, and comrades is the glue, binding us together.

Wong's world outlook is founded on solidarity, a commitment to the radical restructuring of society, and a strong work ethic. And this mind-set is a direct consequence of her externalizing her experience. "Our lives into theory; our theory into action" was a favorite slogan of the Women Writers Union, an activist writing group that originated in the Creative Writing Department at San Francisco State in the '70s. Nellie joined the WWU and met two Radical Women members there who introduced her to socialist feminism.

FAMILY AS A WORKING COMMUNITY

Wong's family was her first community—all of them working at the Great China Restaurant, six days a week. On Wednesday nights, when the restaurant was closed, the family ate a sit-down dinner. They were proud Cantonese Americans, not wealthy by any stretch, and they all became artists, poets, historians, journalists of their people. In this first community, they didn't have much materially—

maybe little Nell would get a new sweater or a pair of new shoes at the beginning of the school year. But she watched and observed and worked. "Stinky Cigarette Uncle (Ah Chew Yen Gung)" and Ah Chenk were added to a loving constellation of family and acquaintances.

From her poetry, you can see how Nellie formed her perspective, and her work ethic, from when she was very little—from when she and her six siblings worked together in the restaurant with her Ma and *Bah Bah* training them and assigning specific responsibilities. "Typing the menu" was one of Nellie's assignments. The kids were not paid but collected tips. So young to be working, so young to understand her role: "knowing that my fingers/helped to support the family,/my secretarial skills a blip/of the family business/known as the Great China Restaurant."[3]

> Typing the menu,
> a job I didn't apply for
> but became mine
> in between making coffee,
> [. . .]
> anxious for tips [. . .]
> understanding, even then,
> that money grew not on trees
> but through our labor" (19)

In "Ironing, Ironing" (13), dedicated to Tillie Olsen, Nellie allows her imagination to roam: from the old radio shows of the '40s and '50s to being betrayed by her body's eczema; from ironing at midnight when her *Bah Bah* drank whiskey and fried his pork chops to the Jacob

Lawrence painting of three Black women ironing; and finally, coming home to her uncle, Ah Chenk, a laundryman, and understanding that "Ironing is honest work" (24).

"Song of Farewell" (11) shows Nellie tenderly washing her Ma's feet while fantasizing an afterlife with her dad. Being Chinese American, Nellie has a dual perspective: she has roots in China that enable her to chronicle the history of racism against the Chinese in America. No nationalist but an internationalist, she embraces the oppressed of the world and honors their courage and tenacity to prevail. As such, she has internalized the incomparable and militant leadership of the most oppressed.

Both as a writer and in her person, Nellie embraces the most energetic, committed, and focused outlook—an optimism, an almost innocence, even. In a world of chaos, war, violence in our streets, and grinding poverty, crisis breeds opportunity, and Nellie points the way—to the thrilling democracy and resistance movements that have sprung up on every continent during the last few years.

BROAD SHOULDERS

To those of us Chinese Americans who grew up on Hollywood movies, wishing we were white like those beautiful movie stars, Joan Crawford or Barbara Stanwyck, Wong's poems, "Love Affair" (91) and "Broad Shoulders" (55), give these films their due.

"Broad Shoulders" is a beautiful meditation on women's strength. In the beginning, the girl-narrator says she wants to be a leader, but she doesn't know how. Over the course of the poem, she grows and learns: "Her shoulders grew so broad, the world entered her mind and her soul" (54). She begins to gain a global perspective that will stay with her, even if she never leaves home, even if she types for the rest of her life, even if she is too afraid to take any risks. She now understands that her desires as a young girl are not going to be fulfilled: "She hungered for fullness and yet she knew her body would never yield a child now. Fullness, she told herself, was not necessarily becoming a mother" (55). As she ages, she regrets: if she had never learned to type, where would her fullness be? If her mother and father had the money to send her to college at seventeen, where would she be now? Not here, in this room, typing after midnight; not here, alone, without husband, without children, without a fire crackling to warm her tender bones . . .

But her shoulders keep growing, and the woman comes to understand that there are other means to fulfillment: "Ma [. . .] Thank you for my broad shoulders. I've never had a chance to tell you that I love you" (57).

Ma's gold tooth was gone [. . .] and the white daisies [. . .] she came home to rest [. . .] Her shoulders would guide her toward fullness [. . .] Her sisters would always be around her: the blood sisters but especially her revolutionary sisters, the ones who spoke out defending her and themselves [. . .], the ones who [. . .] eloquently spoke about the strength and leadership of women workers, lesbians, and women of all colors, women of all ages, women of all nations. These revolutionary sisters, her comrades, with the broadest, most beautiful shoulders of all. She learned from them because her eyes were wide open now. Somehow her eyes had decided to come out from

hiding and nudged her tofu shoulders, firm and yet tender [. . .] she
saw the women, walking shoulder to shoulder, she saw the dark vio-
lets blooming around them as they rose and lifted the world from her
red, red heart. (58)

What original and colorful Asian American imagery—"tofu shoul-
ders, firm and yet tender." Today, Nellie sees women's potential burst-
ing through America's misogyny, racism, violence, and intolerance
—its fostering of greed, competition, and insensitivity to human suf-
fering—in the zero-sum game of patriarchal capitalism. Growing up,
Nellie herself was a victim of Confucianism: she was a worthless girl,
expected to serve her family until she married; then she'd leave—to
live and serve her husband's family, especially her mother-in-law. She
would have to wait to be served until she herself became a mother-in-
law! Luckily, Nellie, and many other Chinese American women,
found the feminist movement, other options, and freedom.

SELF-LOVE VS. NARCISSISM

Nellie's poem, "I Also Sing of Myself," alludes, of course, to Walt Whit-
man, whose *Leaves of Grass* focuses on the poet being one with the
people—a blade of grass: common, equal, democratic:

> The voice. I cannot command it.
> I cannot censor it.
> I sing, sing of myself [. . .]
> My selves merge, then split
> As atoms [. . .]

Slivers of light shower
The universe of aloneness,
The gratitude of breath (124)

The individual and the collective: the individual merges into the collective, becomes one with the collective. There is a big difference between the self-aggrandizement of the narcissist and the self-love of the group of which you are a member. Nellie expresses a hatred for class oppression and a wide-ranging love of her class.

Revolutionary art reflects the contradictions of a crumbling social system. In a period of skepticism and cynicism, Nellie, as revolutionary artist, gives new meaning to terms and phrases—*disinterested friendship, love for one's neighbor, sympathy, empathy*—vulgarized and rendered meaningless by right-wing fundamentalists. Importantly, while embracing her love for people, Nellie will brook no connection to mysticism. If there is a higher being, it is collective humanity.

> Poets are connectors—the real philosophers . . . the primacy of writing lies at what must be said. The creative impulse, for me, is not an escape from reality, but an ascent to what is deeply human, real, political, social, emotional. I think poetry helps to deepen our humanity—to critique it, to explore it—to enable us to live more fully in the face of adversity, discrimination, exploitation. And, yes, war. Poetry celebrates life even when we're not so sure that peace is possible.[4]

One of Nellie's comrades, Sandra, said that she cried when she read Nellie's "I March." She said, "I remember that day. Now it will live on in our radical history. No one else is writing it down. We absolutely need our own historians!"[5] Here, as in other poems—"When

You Walk Up Larkin Street" or "Ode to the Sincere Café"[6] —it is quite obvious that this is a poet who has a definite feeling for our city— our streets, our Cantonese American waiters and restaurants—a love and appreciation for life as it is—an artistic rendering of reality and not a shrinking from it. She takes an active interest in the concrete fluidity of life and writes about it. Even if her reality takes on a surreal quality, as it does in "Loss Climbing the Hills," there is still her preoccupation with life in three dimensions. These older women and the mystery of their backstories are immortalized.

Nellie's unity of vision comes from an active world-attitude and active life-attitude. Her poetry lays the foundation for a collective humanity that will create a society that is above classes; that is incompatible with mysticism, pessimism, and all the other forms of spiritual collapse. It is realistic, active, vitally collectivist, and filled with a limitless creative faith in the future.

> I may not have time to read the poems of the world,
> But we, the people, are the poem, the song,
> the bird that lifts its wings, rising, rising
> against war, toward peace, toward equality,
> toward revolutionary love, toward children
> growing strong, living, breathing free.[7]

Nellie is never didactic, nor rhetorical, for the truth is in the concrete detail, not in sloganeering or generalities. By expressing her own needs, she expresses our needs, our hopes and aspirations; she will fight for the freedom of all mankind to raise itself to heights only the one percent have achieved in the past.

If authority figures have tried to silence Nellie, demoting her for asking too many questions because of her constant thirst for knowledge, denied her an opportunity to go to college—those deprivations pushed her not to lust for self-aggrandizing privileges, but to create a society with ample opportunities for education and union-paying jobs, for all.

BRIDGE TO FREEDOM

A new class cannot move forward without a memory of the most important landmarks of the past. For Asian America, our writers and poets share some common themes, a continuity of creative tradition. For instance, an important aspect of Asian American culture is our *invisibility*. Themes of invisibility and its political consequences pervade our literature. A vivid example is Mitsuye Yamada's "Invisibility is an Unnatural Disaster," which reveals how Asian American women willingly fall into this stereotype.[8] Just as the individual artist passes biologically and psychologically through the history of the race, so too must the overwhelming majority of a new class pass through the entire history of an artistic culture. Asian American writers remark on how often we are not seen as people of color, and how American society in discussing race seems only to acknowledge Black and white people. Nellie's use of her lifelong disability of eczema as a metaphor for wishing to "embroider new skin" is very powerful. Many of us Asian Americans go through this period of self-hatred, wanting to be white.

Nellie's poem, "When I Was Growing Up," eloquently addresses this phenomenon: longing to be white.[9] Often the next stage of evolution is anger, rebellion, asserting our yellowness, our being different; now we write protest literature. And then we come into our own, a maturity, an embracing of the world, so to speak. We become proud Asian Americans, in solidarity with other Asians, even though there probably were hostilities in the old country—but, given our unifying experience under American racism, those hostilities are rendered irrelevant. We will use terms of *solidarity*—like "Asian American" or "Women of Color"—that bind us together across ethnicities, and speak to our collective oppression.

The concept of "The Portrait of the Artist as a Young Woman" is not applicable for the majority of Asian American women writers, primarily because it often has taken us years to realize we even have a voice! Mitsuye Yamada titled her first book "Camp Notes" because she wasn't even sure she was writing poetry!

Nellie's poetry is transitional. She has broken through capitalism's ideology of contempt and hatred for the *Asian hordes*, our working class, especially Yellow Women. She has directly confronted racism and sexism and class exploitation that were/are the mainstays and source of vast profits for the ruling class. Nellie and many other Asian American poets have smashed the old stereotypes and presented a human face of Asian America, worthy of love and admiration for what we look like, sound like; for what our ambitions, sorrows, and deprivations have been; and for what we can expect in the future. How better to break through the stereotypes that racism and sexism have created than by clearly depicting our humanity, our beauty, our language? By immortalizing Cantonese American English in her poetry, Nellie has reclaimed a language we've been taught to call "broken" or "mutilated."

As Lorraine Hansberry said, in reference to what people of color and women most desire—which really is a revolutionary demand: "To be seen as levelly human, that is enough."[10]

> Yes, I'm a very committed person; otherwise I couldn't be a revolutionary feminist, an activist, a poet. When I've had writing blocks, it's usually because I haven't been thinking as deeply as I should. Sometimes I feel like I just need to jump off the world, so to speak. But reality keeps me in check, as well as my love for language, images, and the beauty of being human. Deep in my heart, and through my life experiences, there is no better way to live than to fight for a better world [. . .] I love the idea of making change for the disenchanted, the dispossessed, not in a 'do-good' manner for the sake of being altruistic, but for the possibilities that we humans with our spirit and fortitude can fight for. Writing poems details those challenges.[11]

Nellie's vision bridges the past to the future, by an immersion into the present. The proletariat needs a continuity of creative tradition. Our class cannot begin the construction of a new culture without absorbing and assimilating the elements of the old cultures. The dialectical nature of the dynamic between individualism and collectivism, the interdependence of both, is what we will take from Nellie's poetry—a more complex idea of the human personality—its passions, feelings, and a deeper and more profound understanding of its psychic forces.

R. L. Barnes, writing on behalf of *U.S. History Scene*, in an online dis-
cussion of Black women's leadership in the Civil Rights Movement,
uses the term "Movement Mamas" to describe the intergenerational
mentorships older Black women activists established with young
women just entering the movement.[12] A deep sense of kinship, sis-
terhood, and gender solidarity has developed between the older and
younger generations. These *mothers* set an example of rebellion for
their *children*. By expanding the boundaries of mothering, Move-
ment Mamas extended familial ties while expanding crucial commu-
nity networks. They played a key role in sustaining the culture of re-
sistance, and in serving as brave role models. Ella Baker is a great
example: a leader in the NAACP, the Southern Christian Leadership
Conference, and the Student Nonviolent Coordinating Committee
(especially here, she focused on training young leadership), Ms.
Baker maintained her maiden name, never gave birth, lived inde-
pendently from her husband, and divorced. She also self-identified
as an anti-imperialist. She was definitely an alternative role model.
Moreover, African American Movement Mamas kept up the tradition
of training young women to be leaders, testifying to the violent
racism and sexism of Southern whites, all while simultaneously
helping to lay the legal foundations for desegregation.

Nellie Wong is such a Movement Mama. She has nurtured Asian
American feminist culture through her writing and expanded the
horizon of socialist feminist leadership, enabling the Socialist Revo-
lution, as Engels said, to leap from the kingdom of necessity to the
kingdom of Freedom. These Movement Ma Mas (for Cantonese

Americans, we put the accent on the second syllable of Ma *Ma*) have greatly expanded the boundaries of *mothering*. Leon Trotsky wrote, "Art is a function of the nerves and demands complete sincerity."[13] I believe Trotsky is talking about *authenticity*; that is, how precisely the artist expresses her innermost feelings and thoughts and passions. A careful and caring reader will know immediately if a poet is being dishonest, rhetorical, grandstanding. The poet must be willing to be absolutely truthful and admit thoughts or actions that reveal weaknesses, admit failings.

In so many of her poems, Nellie reveals that at the same time that she loves being Chinese American, describing the fantastically diverse Chinese cuisine and Chinese traditions that comfort and provide feelings of *home*, she also expresses how strong the socialization process is—to get married, have children, work hard and accumulate material wealth—that influenced her from her childhood to her adulthood. By expressing these negative influences in poetry, by objectifying them, she was able to externalize them; and through study, consciousness raising (which she did with her five sisters in the 1970s!), and being a participant, and then, a leader in the Second Wave of the feminist movement, Ms. Wong changed, evolved, and created for herself new options for living a full and engaged life. In "Conversation on the Train to Shanghai," the narrator reveals her feelings about her divorce:

> [Xiao Wu] asks, "When you got your divorce, who wanted it more? Him or you?"
>
> " [. . .] I wanted it more"
>
> " [. . .] It was to save my own life," I answer.

"But you have each other," Xiao Wu says [. . .]

"That is not enough," I say.

"When love is no longer true, it is best to separate.

Then each person can go on with her and his own life."

Xiao Wu tells me that I am strong.[14]

In the 1970s, Nellie and other feminists of color joined, and then furthered, the women's movement, creating new options for themselves that focused on personal autonomy, overturning patriarchal traditions, becoming visible as activists, nurturing young activists—teaching, training, being accessible. The personal is the political and poetry well-suited to express this statement. Nellie discovered an alternative way of life, bucking the centuries-old Confucian tradition of thoroughly oppressing girls and making them appendages of their husbands and slaves to their mothers-in-law, being forever the invisible servant with bound feet. She rose above this centuries-old subordination of women and joined with other budding feminists to build a feminist movement—and wrote about it. This movement allowed a broad range of options for young feminists.

Nellie's *joie de vivre* is obvious in her appreciation of family itself, from the perspective of her feminist imagination, embracing Chinese American culture. Nellie has authentically created a world that is fresh, loving, nurturing, and supportive—from this decaying, destructive, and diseased society. We can see how engaged Nellie is with life. At seventy-nine years old, she is a renaissance woman, interested in everything: she loves movies, TV, good food, jazz, poetry—and, always, the people, especially the hard-working, toiling masses! She has found an alternative way of life that grants fulfillment. She also has had a community of loving family, comrades, sister and brother poets, and several movements (feminist, people of color, Queer, labor) to support her and to fight isolation.

TO ELIMINATE CLASS CULTURE BY MAKING WAY FOR HUMAN CULTURE

Nellie's body of work is focused on her hard-working family and the workers of the world: the communities she's been so much a part of. The working class basis of our culture is its strength. The *urgent* present demands the revolutionary leadership of the worker, her ethic and her vision.

With incredible insight and the artist's focus on detail, Ms. Wong's goal is to eliminate class culture to make way for human culture. The revolutionary artist lays the ground for a new society, but she does so based on the realities of the old society, determined to eliminate class exploitation, with its violence, destruction, and annihilation—indeed, the lot of the most oppressed sectors of our society. Our times may not yet be ready for a new Socialist culture, which we cannot today even imagine, but only the entrance to it. Nellie Wong and other revolutionists are the gatekeepers, pointing the way.

> I know my mother better all the time.
> She lives inside me. Her hands and mine, our fingers,
> knuckly twins. Together we shred
> chicken for Chinese Chicken Salad . . .

knowing that we feed ourselves

'cause Ma taught us

that self-sufficiency

means work

in the kitchen

and out on the streets.[15]

NOTES

1. http://www.radicalwomen.org

2. Nellie Wong, "Revolutionary Love," *HEArt (Human Equity through Art)*, eds. Leslie Anne Mcilroy, et al., Vol. 5, No. 2, Winter 2002 (Pittsburgh, PA), 22.

3. Wong, *Breakfast Lunch Dinner* (San Francisco: Meridien PressWorks, 2012), 19.

4. Wong, "Sisters Say No to War," *HEArt*, 20.

5. Sandra [last name intentionally withheld], in conversation with Nellie Wong, New Valencia Hall, 747 Polk St., San Francisco, May 2013.

6. Wong, "When You Walk Up Larkin Street" and "Ode to the Sincere Café," *Breakfast Lunch Dinner*, 99; 48.

7. Wong, "I March," *Breakfast Lunch Dinner*, 74.

8. Mitsuye Yamada, "Invisibility Is an Unnatural Disaster: Reflections of an Asian American Woman," *This Bridge Called My Back: Writings by Radical Women of Color* (Massachusetts: Persephone Press, 1981), 35–40.

9. Wong, "When I Was Growing Up," *The Death of Long Steam Lady* (Los Angeles: West End Press, 1986), 23–24.

10. Undocumented Hansberry quote recalled by Merle Woo.

11. Wong, "Sisters Say No to War," *HEArt*, 20–21.

12. R. L. Barnes, "Movement Mamas: How Historians Have Examined Women's Struggles in the Long Civil Rights Movement," *US History Scene*, June 28, 2011.

13. Leon Trotsky, "Art and Politics in Our Epoch," *Partisan Review*, 1938, http://www.marxists.org/archive/trotsky/1938/06/artpol.htm

14. Wong, *Breakfast Lunch Dinner*, 41.

15. Wong, "I Know My Mother Better All the Time," *Breakfast Lunch Dinner*, 82–83.

THE SEAMLESS WORLD

MEI-MEI BERSSENBRUGGE'S POETRY

SUEYEUN JULIETTE LEE

There is a seam between the image of a cloud and your view to
    light blue on a ridge under the cloud,
then a seam between your seeing light blue on the horizon and
    seeing infinity in the same space,
embracing the blue. She interprets angles of moving light without
    calculating the coordinates of a cloud
which suddenly appears. Its appearance is a seam with light going
    through, not translucent matter
through which specks of mica shine like little splinters in your
    brain, she calls an interpretation.[1]

I open my essay with this section from Mei-mei Berssenbrugge's poem, "Combustion," from her 1993 Kelsey Street Press release, *Sphericity*, in order to illustrate how her poetry invites us to transect seeing and understanding—to dwell in the space of negotiation between our constantly alighting attention and the dynamic world. In "Combustion," Berssenbrugge calls us to recognize the seams in our perception: to see the "seam" between the image of a cloud and the imagined blue beneath it, to recognize, in turn, the seam between this light blue and the notion of "infinity" in our imaginations. By highlighting these seams, her poem ultimately argues for the seamlessness of human perception. Everything joins together in the mind: experiences and understandings open into ever unfolding, evolving insights.

Delightfully in the piece, suddenly mica emerges "like little splinters in your brain"—a beautiful way of gesturing at how we arrive at an interpretation. Understanding and interpretation appear as the light we identify and can hold to. But can this interpretation accurately represent the whole? Berssenbrugge's poetry vigorously, though also meditatively and subtly, affirms the complex contingencies that undergird our experience of life.

Although her poetry is "about" many things, at heart Mei-mei Berssenbrugge's work explores human consciousness: how do we know what we know; how do we feel what we feel; and how does seeing impact being? Her poetry centers on these questions by investigating the environment, perception, and visual art. This is especially evident in Berssenbrugge's five books from Kelsey Street Press—*Sphericity* (1993), *Endocrinology* (1997), *Nest* (1998), *Four Year Old Girl* (1998), and *Concordance* (2006). Berssenbrugge's poetry reminds us that being is an activity: we are always active in the world; and the world is always active within and around us. Her Kelsey Street books are also essential texts for recognizing her contributions to contemporary experimental writing in the United States. Her work has helped to radically expand our understanding of Asian American literature's possibilities—by informing emergent ecopoetics' discussions, challenging us to dwell more attentively within the porous interchanges between self and world.

Often written in collaboration with visual artists Richard Tuttle or Kiki Smith and representing over a decade of work, Berssenbrugge's

53

Kelsey Street books frequently investigate the body's evolving relationship to the landscape by monitoring the small shifts and transformations in the speaker's attention. These aspects of Berssenbrugge's poetry have led to the dominance of phenomenological frameworks for considering her writing. Though my study will not unseat the critical productivity of these frames, I invite us to consider how recognizing her participation in the budding multiculturalist movement of the 1970s can help us better appreciate the socio-political implications of her work. Her generous, self-reflexive ethics of attention offers powerful possibilities for recalibrating our orientation in a world that insists on affirming divisive visibilities.

Born in Beijing to Dutch and Chinese parents, Berssenbrugge was primarily raised in Massachusetts.[2] After earning her MFA from Columbia University, she traveled extensively in her early twenties, living briefly in Nepal and Alaska before relocating to New Mexico in the mid-1970s. She currently maintains homes in both New York City and northern New Mexico with her husband, visual artist Richard Tuttle.

It's quite apt that Berssenbrugge continues to live between these two sites, as they reflect two poles that orient her work. Berssenbrugge's time as a young student in New York exposed her to the burgeoning multicultural movement and put her in direct contact with other Asian American and multi-ethnic activists and artists. In New Mexico she furthered these conversations and became steeped in a vibrant visual arts community. By engaging with her work through these locations, we can achieve a parallax vision that more richly accounts for her contributions as a contemporary American poet. By attending to these two poles, we can see how Berssenbrugge's innovations give formal expression to her interest in affirming and celebrating difference without stabilizing into essentialist identity politics. Her Kelsey Street books reflect her decisive shift from highlighting racial or ethnic signifiers to focus on the dynamics of consciousness, allowing her to posit the contingencies against which we construct our orientation within and to the broader world.

ORIENTATIONS IN BERSSENBRUGGE'S

CRITICAL RECEPTION

The earliest extant discussion of Berssenbrugge's work appears in a short review by Megan Adams, published in the feminist poetics journal *HOW(ever)* in 1984, in which Adams describes how "the 'objective' stance of scientific language does not dominate [Berssenbrugge] and thus she is free to use its descriptive power without being used by it."[3] Other reviews focus on the subjective qualities of Berssenbrugge's writing. One in particular, Denise Newman's 1992 article, "The Concretion of Emotion: Engaging with Mei-mei Berssenbrugge's *Empathy*," engages its subject by adopting Berssenbrugge's structure and style: the review is written in stanzas composed of long sentences. To make sense of the collection, Newman collages her journal-like reading responses together with quotations from Berssenbrugge's poems. Of Berssenbrugge's art, Newman writes, "[s]eeing is as much in the mind as it is in the organ of sight./Perception is very much based on interpretation rather than a simple reaction to stimuli."[4]

However, literary critic Charles Altieri's phenomenological explication has had the greatest impact for shaping the ongoing reception of Berssenbrugge's work. In his 2002 essay, "Intimacy and Experiment in Mei-Mei Berssenbrugge's *Empathy*," he suggests that "[s]he seeks ways to force us back from narrative and drama to the more elemental phenomenological aspects characterizing how language helps make it possible for us to connect to a world beyond the ego."[5] In order to accomplish this, Berssenbrugge creates what Altieri terms an "imaginative site," a space created by affiliating with the possibility of movement between the self and the world.[6] This space is a construction rather than a precondition and, for Altieri, is a distinctive trait of Berssenbrugge's oeuvre. In *Empathy* (Station Hill Press, 1989), the site is generated along two affective axes: the desire for intimacy and a critique of representation.

Altieri's argument raises an interesting dilemma which Berssenbrugge's poetry seeks to address: how to express the emotive, interior terrains of being without falling into characterizations that limit or flatten the complexities of the subject. Altieri's argument has deep implications for anyone interested in reinvigorating the lyric/subjective mode in poetry. The emotive, when expressed through a reliance on representation, requires fixed objects to provide some stable sense of desire. However, post-modernity has taught us that there is very little in the world that is not in transit, flexible, and multiple. Altieri suggests that Berssenbrugge's poetry offers a solution to this conundrum in terms of an organizational method captured in the conjectural mode. He defines conjecture as "an ongoing process of constant mobile adjustments content with a series of imaginative leaps" (58). This stance requires a continuous, flexible, echoic relationship between the self and world that operates with an intuitive alacrity rather than logical linearity. According to Altieri, "both spatial and temporal access to other persons is best achieved if we can imagine ourselves as cubist painters bringing multiple overlapping perspectives together as a kind of parallax view projecting beyond what can only be dimly realized in specific images" (60).

Other poetics scholars have followed Altieri's model of reading Berssenbrugge through a phenomenological lens, but with different nuances and emphases. In her 2003 article, "Mei-mei Berssenbrugge's *Four Year Old Girl* and the Phenomenology of Mothering," Megan Simpson remarks that Berssenbrugge's "focus on the body and women's experience invites feminist readings of her work," which Simpson then undertakes through a discussion of Berssenbrugge's 1998 collection *Four Year Old Girl.*[7] In Berssenbrugge's poetry, Simpson finds "maternal experience is mediated by discourse as well as her sense that identity is created and recreated in the point of contact between same (self) and other."[8]

Asian American literary scholars have tended to interpret and frame these phenomenological aspects in Berssenbrugge's poetry under the banner of "subjectivity," a term that embraces situated standpoints more explicitly than phenomenology does. The critical visibility of Berssenbrugge's work as "Asian American" concurred with the rise of a mid-1990s Asian American institutional critique of essentialist, stabilized notions of subjectivity. The rising critical interest by Asian American literary scholars in Berssenbrugge's work says a great deal about the optics of institutional visibility, given her active role in the burgeoning Asian American literary movement in New York City during the mid-'70s. For example, Jeannie Chiu's 2004 essay, "Identities in Process: The Experimental Poetry of Mei-mei Berssenbrugge and Myung Mi Kim" seeks to move Berssenbrugge's and Kim's poetry from the margins of consideration in Asian American literary studies, emphasizing how they make "major contributions to contemporary American literature, Asian American literature, and contemporary American poetry."[9] Chiu discusses how Berssenbrugge "challenge[s] not only essentialist notions of ethnic and racial identity, but also the transcendent 'I' of conventional lyric poetry."[10]

Most recently, Joseph Jeon's *Racial Things, Racial Forms* examines Berssenbrugge's work in conversation with visual art through an analysis of her collaborative artist books. Jeon's analysis focuses on the unique physical features of these books. *Hiddenness* (Library Fellows of the Whitney Museum of American Art, 1987) and *Endocrinology* feature a "tail," "a colored bit of paper [that] extends past the bottom margin of the page"[11] that is visible even when the book is shut, as a means for examining Berssenbrugge's positioned phenomenological poetics. (A positioned phenomenology makes the subject's social location as apparent as its existence as an embodied being.) Jeon suggests that the artifactual nature of these artist books "figure positionality itself as a kind of irreducible thingness that opposes the immaterial blankness [...] associated with normative universalism."[12] The physical features of the books and the poetry printed within them work together to "call attention to more contingent, positioned bodies" (78), thereby working to "interrogate the social dynamics of other more complex forms of human interactions, regarding racialization" (79).

Jeon's analysis works to create resonant analogies between racialization processes and the aesthetic strategies Berssenbrugge and her two artist collaborators, Richard Tuttle and Kiki Smith, employ in these books. By inviting a particularized physical encounter with the text through the material qualities of the books as objects, and by producing writing that focuses on the body's engagements with its environment, these collections invite the reader to query "what it means to see difference, in one another and in oneself, without re- ductively recognizing difference as an indelible mark that, like tails extending past the page's margin, we identify without even opening the book" (107). Jeon's interrogation of "thingness" helpfully asserts the positionally phenomenological poetics in Berssenbrugge's work that bridges experimental poetics and Asian American studies' dis- courses for considering her poetry.

My study hardly seeks to overturn the phenomenological basis for reading Berssenbrugge's writing, which is terrifically illuminating. Rather, my hope is that by examining her poetry within the context of the two distinct arts-making communities—New York and New Mexico—that shaped her work, we can better appreciate the degree to which her poems' phenomenal aspects also speak to socio-political orientations. The socio-political, abstracted, and formal aspects of Berssenbrugge's work needn't be isolated from one another. In fact, Berssenbrugge's Kelsey Street Press publications can help us identify the seams and fluencies between these spaces.

NEW YORK / NEW MEXICO

During the 1970s, New York City flowered with numerous, politi- cized multi-ethnic literary communities. These groups emerged from the groundswell of minority students engaged in civil rights and anti-war activism, and include the Nuyorican Poets Cafe and the

Studio Museum of Harlem. Founded in 1971, the Basement Workshop, located in a "damp basement of a Chinatown tenement,"[13] was part of this renaissance, one which sought to coalesce an Asian American cultural and political community through its programming. Though various communities of Asian descent had lived in New York City for nearly a century, Basement Workshop sought to create a coalition of cross-ethnic alliances to foster a strategically self-identified Asian American community, as evidenced by its mission statement:

> Encourag[ing] communication and promot[ing] understanding between Asians in America and Asian Americans and the general American public;
> Stimulating the interest of Asians in America concerning their own welfare;
> Provid[ing] assistance to research projects and programs directly related to the welfare of Asian Americans and particularly those who live in Chinatown.[14]

Asian American cultural history tends to privilege northern California as the dominant site of the 1960s and early '70s Asian American cultural renaissance, locating the movement in student protests for ethnic studies-based courses at San Francisco State University and the University of California, Berkeley. Though a result of these same impulses, Basement Workshop operated outside of a university context and demonstrated its strong community orientation in its programming and location, based in an historic Asian ghetto. Launched by activist and Columbia University graduate student Danny Yung in 1970, Basement Workshop offered courses in English, cultural citizenship, and the creative arts; it also sought to document the Asian American community it served by collecting archival materials and publishing *Bridge* magazine.[15] Because of its dual commitments towards community uplift and arts programming, cultural historian Daryl Joji Maeda finds that Basement Workshop "was arguably the most important Asian American cultural institution on the East Coast."[16] Though Basement Workshop shut down in 1986, it spawned a generation of artists and activists, many of whom would go on to launch other projects and institutions, such as the Asian American Arts Centre.

In its mission to foster literary arts, Basement Workshop attracted a host of younger Asian American authors seeking support and community. In a statement for the "Generations" issue of *The Asian American Literary Review*, poet and fiction writer Richard Oyama recalls, "Though I'd taken creative writing classes at The City College of New York, I longed to share my work with kindred spirits."[17] He also recounts Berssenbrugge among his "youthful mentors." Though not as visible as other Asian American authors and activists at this time, Berssenbrugge was actually quite an active figure at Basement Workshop. In her 2002 interview with Asian American poetics scholar Zhou Xiaojing, Berssenbrugge describes her extensive participation in this historically important community: "In New York at Basement Workshop, I presented my play, 'One, Two Cups,' directed by Frank Chin; several dance collaborations with the Morita Dance Company, directed by Theodora Yoshikami; and many workshops."[18]

Through Basement Workshop, Berssenbrugge interacted with some of the central figures of the Asian American cultural renaissance and developed strong friendships with them. In that same interview with Xiaojing, Berssenbrugge stated, "I lived for a while in San Francisco, near Frank [Chin] and his wife Kathleen Chang, who was my friend, a performance artist, a visionary and the subject of my play. I was included in the *Aiiieeeee! Anthology*.[19] Although abstraction, philosophy, and the visual arts began to take more of my attention, many of these friendships continue."[20]

These relationships and interests led Berssenbrugge to interact and network with other multi-ethnic and activist writers. She recalls how "the poet Michael Harper invited me to a conference of multicultural writers in Madison, Wisconsin in 1973 . . . I met and became friends with Frank Chin, Shawn Wong, Lawson Inada, Simon Ortiz, Al Young, and most importantly Ishmael Reed and Leslie Silko. This was a fervent, pioneering period of asserting and defining multicultural writing in America and it was fantastically exciting" (200).

After relocating to New Mexico, Berssenbrugge continued to seek out and work with writers and artists who shared her interest in creating alliances and fostering new work. In New Mexico, she taught writing at the Institute of American Indian Arts in Santa Fe, along with Arthur Sze and Phillip Foss, who "started a magazine that [they] all worked on, called *Tyuonyi*" (200). *Tyuonyi* was published from 1985–1998 and brought together work by a variety of multiethnic and experimental authors. In his presentation at SUNY Rochester in 2010, Sze described how *Tyuonyi* was named after the Pueblo dialect Keresan word that meant "Meeting Place." They hoped to "braid different literary aesthetics and to bring them into conversation."[21]

The term "multiculturalism" emerged from the various civil rights and race protests of the late '60s and '70s. Multiculturalism distinguishes itself from cultural nationalism in its strong ties to public education and its goal of producing an inclusive American public sphere (rather than a radical break from it). In this regard, it is more closely tied to the early civil rights' efforts of the '50s, "when the black objective, through the entire course of the struggle in the courts of the 1940s and 1950s for equality, was assimilation."[22]

Rather than simply enfolding racialized minorities into the dominant culture, though, multiculturalism sought to revalue diversity, making difference central, rather than obstructionist, to a new American national identity. It intended to represent and celebrate both the diversity and legitimacy of a decidedly ethnic citizenry, and as such has strong ties to social justice movements. This is particularly apparent in the emergent Asian American discourses of the period. For example, multicultural writing of the '70s (now considered cultural nationalist, rather than multicultural) was frequently characterized by vigorous assertions of the writer's ethnic identity and protest spirit, reflected in early Asian American collections such as the 1971 *Roots: An Asian American Reader*, printed by the Asian American Studies Center at UCLA, and *Aiiieeeee! An Anthology of Asian-American Writers* (Howard University Press, 1974). Despite its vigorous denunciations of racial injustice, at the heart of multiculturalism (as it was then understood) lay an ultimately utopian vision for a country that could see beyond race while valuing differences.

Since then, the term has undergone a transformation of meaning. As literary scholar Timothy Yu notes, the ethnic literatures spawned by multiculturalist efforts eventually gained wide acceptance in the mainstream, primarily because of "the sincere, personal voice, its immediacy, its artlessness,"[23] which became the standard mode of expression. Protest writing gave way to what Yu terms the "MFA mainstream," the production of lyric writing whose utopian celebration of difference ultimately aestheticized and de-politicized social critique. For example, in her seminal Asian American cultural study *Immigrant Acts: On Asian American Cultural Politics* (Duke University Press, 1996), Lisa Lowe found that intergenerational conflicts between immigrant parents and native-born children frequently displaced social and political histories of racial oppression. The result was that the strident multiculturalism of the '70s transformed into a commodified mainstream in the '80s as its emphasis moved from "politics to 'verbal beauty.'"[24]

Despite multiculturalism's later cooptation, it still contributed meaningfully to the development of Berssenbrugge's poetics. Her assertion of her personal relationship with artists such as Kathleen Chang and Leslie Marmon Silko further indicates her connection to these early multiculturalist values, which assert difference while affirming a deeply universal humanism. We can see how these values were a central aspect of Berssenbrugge's early poetry. Her first full-length collection, *Summits Move with the Tide* (Greenfield Review Press, 1974), offers a cross-section of the various cultures and landscapes that shaped her young adulthood. Importantly, Berssenbrugge chose to include her short play, "One, Two Cups," in this debut collection. This play explores family history and also demonstrates her connection to Basement Workshop and the burgeoning Asian American community. Many of these early poems include a short line noting where they were composed—Ios in Greece; Bhauda, Nepal; and the Naran Valley in Pakistan—indicating an expansive openness to diverse cultures. Through this first collection, we can appreciate the degree to which Berssenbrugge shared multiculturalist sentiments. Furthermore, the atmosphere of the early multiculturalist movement promoted sharing, exploration, and collaboration, practices which continue to inform her work and are strongly present in her Kelsey Street Press books.

Berssenbrugge's Kelsey Street period followed the release of her groundbreaking collection, *Empathy*, and reflects the maturation and full exploration of this mode in her writings. *Empathy* is Berssenbrugge's self-acknowledged "breakthrough" collection. Formally, her mature work is recognizable for its long lines and a preference for the poem in series over the short, lyrical pieces characteristic of her early writing. Despite stylistic differences between her early and more mature poems, her later work continues to demonstrate Berssenbrugge's commitment to affirming and exploring culturally diverse spaces.

For example, in the very first section of *Empathy*, we move from the waterfront in Sydney, Australia, to the Temple of Heaven in Beijing, to the very easternmost edge of Arctic Alaska, then to the Southwestern desert. However, her interest in these locations isn't limited to their cultural contexts, though these contexts certainly do play a role. In *Empathy*, Berssenbrugge begins to explore the dynamic relationship between the environment and human consciousness. These poems suggest how landscapes permeate, and are permeated by, our attention. Her later work further centers upon and explores this theme.

Importantly, Berssenbrugge's stylistic transformation coincided with her relocation to New Mexico in the mid 1970s. In the desert, one must be particularly mindful of the environment—with little ground cover, storms and other weather patterns are particularly impressive, and the changing intensity of sunlight over the course of the day often dictates one's activities and mobility. It is precisely this quality of light—along with the dramatic valleys, bluffs, and mountains dotting the landscape—that has lured visual artists and painters to the region for years.

Paintings by its most famous denizen artist, Georgia O'Keeffe, with whom Berssenbrugge briefly associated, have a metonymic relationship to the region. Indeed, a fuller understanding of Berrsenbrugge's poetics requires us to attend to the visual artists she worked with and befriended in the Southwest, and how they influenced her writing. By situating her as an engaged participant in New Mexico's visual arts communities, we can see how many of her poetic innovations can be better understood as emerging out of the shared nexus of interests inflecting the work of many artists from this region, including Georgia O'Keeffe and Agnes Martin. When viewed together, despite their external differences, these women's works share abiding interests in perception, consciousness, and the environment. Whereas O'Keeffe's gestural paintings imbue the landscape with a strong subjective stance and emotional presence, Martin works far more directly in the idiom of abstraction. Insofar as Berssenbrugge's poetry condenses emotions into atmospheres with abstracted, sometimes philosophical meditations, it shares tendencies with both painters.

Berssenbrugge not only lived near O'Keeffe, she worked briefly as her associate shortly before the famed painter's death. Berssenbrugge's relationship with Martin was far more intimate. Martin was a friend and mentor to Berssenbrugge's husband, Richard Tuttle, with whom she shared a retrospective exhibition at the Modern Art

Museum at Fort Worth, Texas, in 1998. In a personal comment to me, Berssenbrugge described how the first person she introduced her newborn daughter to directly out of the hospital was Agnes Martin.

Though Berssenbrugge never formally produced published work with either O'Keeffe or Martin, her move to the Southwest coincides with her increased interest in the visual, which is captured in several ongoing collaborations with visual artists Tuttle and Smith. I'd like us to consider these collaborative works as being in conversation with a more broadly considered New Mexico visual arts community that was invested in exploring the environment and perception. For example, Berssenbrugge once stated, "you cannot live in New Mexico and not be visually dominant."[25] Though Berssenbrugge considers *Empathy* her breakthrough work, the seeds for this new mode first appeared in poems composed for an earlier 1987 collaboration, *Hiddenness*, with Richard Tuttle. Joseph Jeon's analysis of *Hiddenness* illustrates how these collaborations are able to fruitfully center on shared but diverse visual practices. He notes that where *Hiddenness* ostensibly "places the visual and the verbal at odds,"[26] it actually presents "two kinds of visuality"(83), bridging the way we observe the visual characteristics of text on a page with its recognized meaning.

Berssenbrugge's Kelsey Street Press publications allow us to identify how New York and New Mexico orient and shape her poetics, which strides neatly between these spaces. If New York city reflects her multiculturalist commitments, then I suggest New Mexico illuminates her interests in the environment and visuality. We can especially see the latter aspects at work in her first Kelsey Street Press book and second collaboration with Tuttle. *Sphericity* is comprised of six poems titled after various abstract concepts: "Ideal," "Size," "Combustion," "Sphericity," "Experience," and "Value." Interleaved with watercolors by Tuttle, the poems share the same titles. *Sphericity* was written just before and after [their daughter] Martha's birth: "I was interested that the changes in body chemistry so dramatically changed my language and perception, during this time."[27]

Nearly each poem in *Sphericity* begins with a visual consideration:

I did not know beforehand what would count for me as a new color.[28]

Given the depth of the colors of the mineral, whose source is an
    oscillation of spaces or volumes of energy, as a pink ray of light
    and rose coils of it [. . .][29]

Your description of the amaryllis, projective, imaginary, and sym-
    bolic, still corresponds to you [. . .][30]

These visual aspects shift seamlessly into abstractions that take on emotional content: "The significance of a bird flying out of grapes in a store relates to the beauty of the color of the translucency of grapes."[31] Throughout these pieces, Berssenbrugge's primary interest is in finding resonances and fluencies, identifying how what we see transforms into internalized experience.

Two particles that make a continuum or ideal in how the space
    between them relates to a third event,
as how clouds against a windowpane admit space that continues to
    a cloud on the mountain,
a sheath of a space of feeling in material sheaths of her body for a
    perceived order, depend
on your having felt the relation. A horizon forms around his voice
    through which no sound can pass.[32]

Above, objects continue to move and transform in relation to each other, and their relation emerges as the "ideal" against which emotional experience is cast. Two particles transform into shifting cloud light on a windowpane, which echo with the speaker's internal organization of the world. Her sense of the cloud's visual limits, embodied in her experience of "his voice," becomes its own horizon. This section delicately points to structures of love.

As demonstrated above, a central feature of Berssenbrugge's work is the long line. These long lines can be viewed as a formal strategy for infiltrating the imagined seams between thought, self, and world. As critic and poet Ben Lerner wrote in his 2006 *Rain Taxi* review of Berssenbrugge's collected poems, *I Love Artists* (University of California Press, 2006), "The radical extension of Berssenbrugge's line heightens the reader's awareness of time and space by making the reader aware that time and space are running out: the far right margin is a precipice. Perhaps this is why Barbara Guest has described Berssenbrugge's line as 'perilous.'"[33]

The "peril" of Berssenbrugge's poetry is that it draws the reader's attention to the very limits of perception, inviting us to observe the subtle shifts and grains in how we observe the world and our place in it. Such an enterprise hovers in an ambiguous space that is both central to, and on the margins of, cognition and subjectivity. To be alert, and aware, in the manner that Berssenbrugge's poetry invites us to be, requires in some sense a relinquishment of our sense of self.

Berssenbrugge's use of the long line shares key affinities with Language poetry. In his seminal 1993 essay, "Parataxis and Narrative," Bob Perelman describes how parataxis is the "dominant mode of postindustrial experience,"[34] in which atomized, continual bursts of narrative, whether in new media forms or through the hypersaturation of advertisements in public spaces, inundate our daily lives. Parataxis places coherent semantic units in series without delineating a hierarchical relationship between them. Experientially, we associate parataxis with fragmentation and the loss of meaning. The New Sentence, initially coined by Ron Silliman, seeks to reclaim paratactical structures in order to elongate and stretch our appreciation of meaning's contingencies by developing new understandings out of an accretive, rather than a narrative, reading experience. Each individual sentence, often seen as discontinuous from what precedes and follows it, in fact works in relation to the entire series and "encourages attention to the act of writing and to the writer's particular position within larger social frames."[35] These sentences "imply continuity and discontinuity simultaneously."[36]

Where many texts, such as Lyn Hejinian's *My Life* and Ron Silliman's *Ketjak*, work in large prose blocks under the Language umbrella, Berssenbrugge's continued use of line and section breaks make strong use of white space, thereby lending the composition a more meditative reading experience while conjuring up stronger lyric sentiments in its visual presentation. The self, though ambient —surfacing as a pronoun within the surround—remains central to Berssenbrugge's writing. Whereas Language poets often used parataxis as a means to semantically intervene in capitalism's means-end rationality, Berssenbrugge's long sentences work trans-culturally— by recognizing relationships across socially imagined differences, whether racial, environmental, or conceptual, in order to offer one seamless, semantically unified whole. In a 2003 interview with Laura Hinton, Berssenbrugge stated, "I would say that the ethos and aesthetic of my poetry aspire to be holistic, continuous, or one thing."[37] Her long lines reflect her desire to "dissolv[e] borders,"[38] thereby allowing one's perception to traverse multiple territories: from the interior and emotional, to the self-consciously perspectival, to an attentiveness to atmosphere required by landscapes and geographies.

It is also through Berssenbrugge's long line that we can identify seams between the New York and New Mexico aspects of her work. Her ability to orient the self and simultaneously explore the contingencies at work in constituting selfhood are heightened by the way she weaves together analytical commentary, lived experience, and visual description. This structure is particularly evident in *Nest*, 1998 winner of the Asian American Lifetime Achievement Award for Literature. Now in its third printing (2014), *Nest*'s continued success amply demonstrates Berssenbrugge's legibility and importance to the Asian American literary community.

In *Nest*, the optimism of bridging various cultures and spaces which characterized Berssenbrugge's work takes on a more critical perspective, highlighting the challenging ambiguities at work in racialized experience. In this text in particular, her interest in visuality actively enfolds examinations into the limitations of racialization structures, which rely on optics. For example, the titular poem, "Nest," is dedicated to postcolonial feminist theorist Gayatri Spivak. Composed in five sections, each line of the poem is a single sentence that weaves together inquiries into origins, motherhood, language, and place. Throughout the piece, the motif of the nest emerges to suggest gendered, racialized experience: "The foreign woman occupies a home that's impersonal, like the nest of a parasite."[39] The nest invokes a made environment that one builds into a home, but in the poem also connotes foreignness. In a nest, elements of the environment are woven together to create a new structure—in this case, a domestic space, one which circulates various languages: Chinese, a possible second "local language," and the implied English of the speaker's current location and child.

> My mother tongue, Chinese, has an immemorial history before me.
> I was inserted into it, a motive for my language.
> I learned it naturally, filling it with intentions, and will leave it without intent for other children. (45)

The woman's domestic imagination is interlaced with descriptions of her experience of language. As a speaking subject, she filled her "mother tongue" with agency—"a motive," licensed by her natural relationship to it as a native speaker. Later, this experience of language transforms: "Change of mother tongue between us activates an immunity, margin where dwelling and travel are not distinct" (46). To change mother tongues is to find oneself in flight and to take on dynamism as a central tenet of being. In the poem, this shift ostensibly lends itself to an "immunity"—from what?—but later in the piece we can see how this results in particular challenges:

> Speaking, an artifact, creates a loophole for no rapport, no kinship, no education, on a frontier where wild is a margin of style, and rhetoric's outside that. [. . .] Speech opens on a lost plain, then contracts to a diffuse margin between metaphor for space and concept of drunk, ill, running away. (49)

The fraught experience of language as a "loophole," in which there can be no relation, calls to mind Spivak's assertion that subaltern speech cannot be heard by subalternizing systems. Such speech becomes symbolically excessive. It runs away, evading understanding. The poem suggests that the immunity of the shifting mother tongue is precisely that of flight and excess, which can lead to a challenging isolation—a lost plain.

The poem concludes without a clear resolution to this conundrum of language, but suggests movement through visibility:

> So, I speak with care, but prove authority won't take me far,
>   because the area's too large.
> In this, daughter, you see more than I did at your age, because you
>   see me. (49)

The daughter sees more because she sees her mother's authority, doubled here in the sense of parental power and authorship. Berssenbrugge's concluding turn towards visuality demonstrates how modes of sight lead directly to the generation of knowledge and potential action. By witnessing her mother's authority, however far it fails to go, the daughter sees "more," implying other possibilities in her future.

Berssenbrugge's work makes important contributions to twentieth-century American poetry through its stylistic innovations. Her increasing recognition as a major Asian American poet is also well-deserved and timely. By leaving aside fixed or definitional understandings of identity, in favor of a highly nuanced attention to space and self, Berssenbrugge is able to soften our imagination of the boundaries that differentiate the self from the world. As a poet,

Berssenbrugge invites us to encounter and dwell in seamlessness, requiring a new mode of attentiveness. Her work posits that to be alive and perceptive is to be active: meaning is constantly created by our ongoing negotiations within and to the world.

I also want to acknowledge the important role that community plays in avant-garde Asian American poetry. Authors of this particular cohort are regularly grouped together, despite their geographical and social differences. Although avant-garde Asian American authors, such as Theresa Hak Kyung Cha and John Yau, frequently worked outside of, or peripheral to, more established or recognizable Asian American communities, they were often deeply embedded in other social circles that informed their writing. A better understanding of these other communities can enrich our appreciation for the formal contributions made by these authors through their work. Berssenbrugge is particularly notable for her early engagement with, and contributions to, the budding Asian American literary community in New York, and for how her later writing continues to develop her earlier commitments to diversity and subjectivity.

By reading Berssenbrugge's work in the context of the various arts-making communities she engaged with in New York and New Mexico, we can also see how her interests in diversity, language, subjectivity, and the environment, lead her to develop her poetic innovations. I am particularly attentive to her time at the Basement Workshop in New York and the visual arts community in Taos. Because Berssenbrugge's poetry is predominantly read within the framework of formal experimentation, the political implications of her poetry are often relegated to an aesthetic level of experience that then percolates down into her readers' social consciousness. By uncovering

74

the interests shaping the creative communities she circulated in, my hope is to highlight the often deeply political interests that informed her experiments. Her poetry subtly invites and challenges us to recognize the seamless contours of experience, highlighting the way our conceptions in turn shape and can transform experience, and vice versa. May her own work be read with this same generous attentiveness to continuities, contingencies, and new possibilities.

NOTES

1. Mei-mei Berssenbrugge and Richard Tuttle, "Combustion," *Sphericity* (Berkeley: Kelsey Street Press, 1993), 21.

2. Xiaoping Yen, "Mei-mei Berssenbrugge," in *Asian American Poets: A Bio-Bibliographical Critical Sourcebook*, ed. Guiyou Huang (Westport: Greenwood Press, 2002), 45.

3. Megan Adams, "Mei-mei Berssenbrugge and the Uses of Scientific Language," *HOW(ever)* 1.3 (February 1984), http://www.asu.edu/pipercwcenter/how2journal/archive/print_archive/alerts0284.html#meimei.

4. Denise Newman, "The Concretion of Emotion: An Analytic Lyric of Mei-mei Berssenbrugge's *Empathy*," *Talisman* 9 (Fall 1992), 122.

5. Charles Altieri, "Intimacy and Experiment in Mei-mei Berssenbrugge's *Empathy*," in *We Who Love to Be Astonished: Experimental Women's Writing and Performance Poetics*, ed. Laura Hinton and Cynthia Hogue (Tuscaloosa: Univ. of Alabama Press, 2002), 55.

6. Ibid., 56.

7. Megan Simpson, "Mei-mei Berssenbrugge's *Four Year Old Girl* and the Phenomenology of Mothering," *Women's Studies: An Interdisciplinary Journal* 32 (2003), 478.

8. Ibid., 481.

9. Jeannie Chiu, "Identities in Process: The Experimental Poetry of Mei-

mei Berssenbrugge and Myung Mi Kim," in *Asian North American Identities Beyond the Hyphen*, ed. Eleanor Ty and Donald C. Goellnicht (Bloomington: Indiana Univ. Press, 2004), 84.

10. Ibid., 85.

11. Joseph Jeon, "Racial Things, Racial Forms: Objecthood" in *Avant-Garde Asian American Poetry* (Iowa City: Univ. of Iowa Press, 2012), 71.

12. Ibid., 75.

13. William Wei, *The Asian American Movement* (Philadelphia: Temple Univ. Press, 1993), 186.

14. Cristiana Baik, "The Basement Workshop Collective," posted in *Open City*, July 9, 2011, http://openthecity.org/?p=3687

15. Alexandra Chang, "Basement Workshop," Grove Art Online, Oxford Art Online, Oxford Univ. Press, http://www.oxfordartonline.com.libproxy.temple.edu/subscriber/article/grove/art/T2094011

16. Daryl Joji Maeda, *Rethinking the Asian American Movement* (New York: Routledge, 2012), 87.

17. Richard Oyama, "The Blithe Country," *Asian American Literary Review* (Spring 2012). Reprinted online by Discover Nikkei: Japanese Migrants and Their Descendants, June 17, 2012, http://www.discovernikkei.org/en/journal/2012/6/17/forum-richard-oyama/

18. Xiaojing Zhou, "Blurring the Borders Between Formal and Social Aesthetics: An Interview with Mei-mei Berssenbrugge," *MELUS 27.1* (2002), 200.

19. Berssenbrugge was actually included in the second anthology edited by Frank Chin, *The Big Aiiieeeee!*, in 1991.

20. Zhou, "Blurring the Borders," 200.

21. Arthur Sze, speaking for the Neilly Series at the University of Rochester on April 22, 2010, Youtube video 9:39, posted by "UniversityRochester," May 18, 2010, http://www.youtube.com/watch?v=IHoq9JOeuAo&list=PL1F88C21D784B3A6&index=1

22. Nathan Glazer, "School Wars: A Brief History of Multiculturalism in America," *The Brookings Review* 11.4 (Fall 1993), 18.

23. Timothy Yu, "Form and Identity in Language Poetry and Asian American Poetry," *Contemporary Literature* 41.3 (2000), 429.

24. Ibid., 435.

25. Zhou, "Blurring the Borders," 200.

26. Jeon, "Racial Things, Racial Forms," 82.

27. Author statement published on the back cover of *Sphericity*.

28. Berssenbrugge and Tuttle, "Ideal," *Sphericity*, 9.

29. Ibid., "Combustion," 19.

30. Ibid., "Value," 39.

31. Ibid., "Ideal," 9.

32. Ibid., 10.

33. Ben Lerner, "Review of Mei-mei Berssenbrugge's *I Love Artists*," *Rain Taxi*, online edition, Summer 2006, http://www.raintaxi.com/online/2006 summer/berssenbrugge.shtml

34. Bob Perelman, "Parataxis and Narrative: The New Sentence in Theory and Practice," *American Literature* 65.2 (June 1993), 313.

35. Ibid., 316.

36. Ibid.

37. Laura Hinton, "Three Conversations with Mei-Mei Berssenbrugge," *Jacket 27* (April 2005), http://jacketmagazine.com/27/hint-bers.html

38. Michèle Gerber Klein, "Mei-Mei Berssenbrugge," *BOMB* 96 (Summer 2006), http://bombsite.com/issues/96/articles/2835

39. Mei-mei Berssenbrugge, "Nest" in *Nest* (Berkeley: Kelsey Street Press, 2003), 47.

SPECULATIVE NOTES

ON BHANU KAPIL'S

MONSTROUS/CYBORGIAN/

SCHIZOPHRENIC POETICS

DOROTHY WANG

Human. Nonhuman. Atavistic. Futuristic. Pre-. Post-. Normal. Monstrous. White. Asian.

How does one begin writing when the "I" who speaks emanates from a body that is viewed *a priori* as a not-citizen, a not-person, a not-human? How to write when the "I" cannot contain the psychic fragments shattered by dislocation, emigration, immigration, and assimilation?

Bhanu Kapil's four books—*The Vertical Interrogation of Strangers* (Kelsey Street Press, 2001), *Incubation: A Space for Monsters* (Leon Works, 2006), *Humanimal: A Project for Future Children* (2009), and *Schizophrene* (Nightboat Books, 2011)—are anchored by the presence of first- and second-person pronouns. Yet this "I", is neither the jaunty O'Haraesque "I do this, I do that" persona nor the evacuated or "erased" subject of Conceptual writing (whose presence nonetheless is felt in the very privilege of voluntary erasure):

I'm going to New York!

(what a lark! what a song!)

where the tough Rocky's eaves

hit the sea. Where th'Acro-

polis is functional, the trains

that run and shout! the books

that have trousers and sleeves![1]

(Frank O'Hara, "Song [I'm going to New York!]," 1951)

Neon in daylight is a

great pleasure, as Edwin Denby would

write, as are light bulbs in daylight.

I stop for a cheeseburger at JULIET'S

CORNER. Giulietta Masina, wife of

Federico Fellini, è bell' attrice.

And chocolate malted. A lady in

foxes on such a day puts her poodle

in a cab.

There are several Puerto

Ricans on the avenue today, which

makes it beautiful and warm.[2]

(O'Hara, "A Step Away from Them," 1956)

I think they do a nice job a the at our dry cleaner. Look at how nice
this shirt is. They do a good job, don't they? Did you ever get paid
from Yale? Did you ever get paid from what's her name, Ardele?
What? They can't pay you? This is a different strike? This is a differ-
ent strike than Kathy's thing? Oy vey. This boy is wired. Look at me,
you can never even tell it's a mic. This boy is wired. Oh, you should

tell Steven, by the way, also that the FMU I gotta get him one of the playlists and he was on the top the playlist officially came out and he was like one of the very top playlist. I gotta give him an official thing, yeah. He did really well at FMU. It's unbelievable. It's yeah. Well, do you like the CD? I gotta really listen to it. Yeah, I mean, people at the station just went apeshit for it.[3]

Identity, for one, is up for grabs. Why use your own words when you can express yourself just as well by using someone else's? And if your identity is not your own, then sincerity must be tossed out as well.[4]

What would it mean to have writing be sincere, yet "not prone to the illusions of a 'stable or essential "me"'?"[5] What does it mean for an "I" to be destabilized yet always connected to something larger— in space (geographic, diasporic) and time (national and global and familial histories)?

But this is to individuate a common sorrow in the time extending from August 1947 to the present era, which is already past.[6]

What would it mean to travel and not be in control of the itinerary? How might movement in space not be a lark or a song?

New Delhi

Oman

London

Denver

Hamburg

Iowa City

Idaho

Florida Keys

Florence, Oregon

"*I don't exist*," says the speaker in *Schizophrene* (32).

The Asian immigrant body, the Asian (American) female body rendered invisible, erased. Cyborgian, machine-like ("technically gifted but not very creative"), nonhuman, yet simultaneously primitive, atavistic, dirty. A humanimal. Two disparate creatures fused together. Mutants. Wolf-children. Siamese twins. Chang and Eng. Medical "curiosities." Monsters. Ghosts. Freaks. Fu Manchu.

"Who doesn't want a perfect [white] body?"[7]

"I said, 'What is a monster?' You said: 'Anybody different'" (16).

Who is "normal"? Someone who eats at a restaurant called Country Buffet (8)? Or drinks chocolate malteds?

The universal poetic speaker, the transparent "I" whose every mundane perception (whether exuberant or melancholy) is received as a brilliant aperçu, is not someone named Laloo. Or Bhanu.

The "Puerto Ricans" are spoken for but they add such nice tropical weather. Now the weather of England is another matter.

81

I was walking home to school after coming home for lunch, and I saw her, an Asian woman of some kind, murmuring. We lived at that time in a white neighborhood but sometimes you encountered them, flecks and drifts of free-able matter.[8]

A step away from *them*

Glasgow

New Jersey

Boston

Maidenhead, England

Jaipur

New York City

Las Vegas

Because it is psychotic not to know where you are in a national space (41).

Or a poetic space.

The poetic speaker, not as the mid-century white male figure of lyric expressivity or the hip white boy of Conceptual writing but as the traumatized diasporic, the schizophrenic, the depressive, the psychotic, the paranoid, the alien, the unassimilated, the unassimilable, the humanimal, the Asian girl.

Somatic forms of memory.[9]

A scar is memory.[10]

The shared vowel is O. A "kind of mouth" (7). The "pilgrim's scream."[11]

The void.

The evacuated center.

Oral and vaginal.

What is a girl? It is an ancient office.[12]

Office, orifice.

What if the personality of the poetic speaker does not sparkle with the insouciant *jouissance* of the *flâneur* or the clever indifference of the (white male) "uncreative writer" but is anhedonistic? Who has the privilege to feel pleasure?

Femaleness as a job. Female pleasure as a (paid) performance.

"My life as a woman" (87).

I wrote another book like a blue lake then drained it, to write from a dip. I am writing to you from depression, from a body of black cloud through which a bird's shadow passes, like a knife.[13]

Can "flatness" of tone be a form of poetic and political rebellion? An insurrection from within. The poem's refusing to rise to the occasion. *Nothing to go apeshit for.*

83

More personality, please.

Why bother if even the "normal" Asian immigrant or racialized other, like the Asian female, is always already pathologized?

The coast of Wales. Your legs were a brown and silver frame to the day: bony, skinny really, and smashed-up looking beneath a coat of coarse, black hair. The sand was white, as were the other holidayers. I felt bitterly the contrast of our own exposed skin against the blueness of the sky and the waves. Your legs were frankly an embarrassment: visible chunks of flesh taken from your thighs and shins at another point in history. Mummy's bright yellow sari with its schizophrenic border of green and black zig-zags, and so on. Only in the water were you and I a family: colorless, wavy and child-centered. Invisible to the eyes of the other families. Do you remember? (50–51)

When I was a child returning to London after a year in India, the children on my street asked me if it was true. "Did you eat snakes for breakfast?" As a joke, I said yes and for a summer or so read books in my garden, shut out from their games: "little black pig," "Paki snake-eater," and so on. When I grew up, I wrote about the bloodstream of a child as intermingling with that of an animal. (40)

You're disgusting.[14]

Is there an English and American poetics that accounts for this pathologized "I"—not the universal speaker but the unloved speaker? Is there a "you" that can meet this (anti-)narrative halfway?

I am writing to you.[15]

Nangal, India

Elizabeth, New Jersey

Columbus, Ohio

Buffalo, New York

Chicago

Paris

New Mexico

Utah

Atlanta

San Diego

Dear friend, where did I go? Where am I going? When you read my palm, it's as if you are hypnotizing my biology. Does a reader hypnotize a writer as much as the other way, the normal way, around? (13)

Is language a lifeboat or a prison?

These are bonds. This is paper.[16]

Grammar is emotional (72).

Nouns are magical to an immigrant, fundamental to a middle-class education (62).

The route to semi-human (cyborgian) status necessitates the mastery of English; otherwise, one undoubtedly remains a monster:

anti-immigrant xenophobia assimilation

"The monster is that being who refuses to adapt to her circumstances."[17]

A monster is always itinerant (87).

"Cyborgs are built for assimilation into households and factories" (12).

capitalism assembly-line labor

Assimilation is a technology of growth (91).

Will she be the wolf-girl who dies (Amala) or the wolf-girl (Kamala) who survives? "In the moonlight, the wolves and their companions were whitish, with eyes that shone when they turned towards him, mildly, reflexively. Blue."[18]

Midnapure, India

Yellowstone

Big Sur

Beatrice, Nebraska

Houston

Maine

Kansas

The Black Hills

The vanishing savage.

What if her tongue becomes "[d]amaged from her travels"?[19]

movement

This was monstrous: the inability to assimilate, on the level of the (im)*migration*
sense, an ordinary experience of weather. Here is the tongue, for ex-
ample, constantly darting out to feel the air: what is it? Is it summer?
Is it a different season? It's a different day. (9–10)

Even if the female Asian (American) writer assimilates the weather
of English, her book is not one of the "books that have trousers and
sleeves!":

On the *night* I knew my book *had failed*, I threw it—in the form of
a *notebook*, a hand-written final *draft*—into the garden of my *house*

in Colorado. Christmas Eve, *2007*. It snowed that *winter* and into the *spring*; before the weather turned truly *warm*, I retrieved my *notes*, and began to write again, from the *fragments, the phrases and lines* still legible on the warped, *decayed* but curiously rigid *pages*.[20]

Yet, in the end, like a miracle, the notebooks and fragments do persist. Like the borders of nation-states, the borders of national poetry-states are not entirely impermeable. And even if a non-citizen cannot find entrance by way of the usual papers—visas, affidavits, and passports—the hitchhiking Asian female poet might still point her thumb towards a project for "future poetics," which her notebooks, weather-beaten and fragmented as they are, limn.

> . . . the right way to go/continue, which is difficult to know for sure, hitchhiking there in the fabulous world that values correctness above sorrow.[21]

The past and the future co-exist in the form of the spectral, the pre- and the post- but also the feral.

> This is a text to do that. Vivify. . . . This is revision, a re-telling of planar space.[22]

> Even the aeroplane's dotted line on the monitor as it descends to Heathrow is a purely weird ambient energy.[23]

Poetry was and is never just the well-wrought urn or the "managerial" handling of language in the digital age. The "I" was never just the individual de-linked from history.

88

Partition and its *trans-generational* effects . . . (i)

Lahore

Calais

Boulder

Like paisley. Flecks and drifts of freeable matter.

. . . a Muslim man with a thick Yorkshire accent . . . (38)

In the airport as the sea. In the forest near Hamburg as *en route*. In northern Colorado with its dark brown fields, a fresh snow sparkling and linear in the furrows. (60)

It was never not about language for schizophrenic (non-white) writers. As for normal *auteurs*.

Like a sentence.[24]

Like a girl.

Schizophrenia is rhythmic.[25]

What is it to make a book "that barely said anything"? To offer the quality of touch?

But this slow, too-dark softness of the light-coming-into-things reminds me of London mornings, when you wake up and go straight out to get *The Guardian* from Balfours for your dad. Taking the way back home through the park, which is heavy with the chocolate and silver stripes of the wet bark of plum trees.[26]

India

suburbs of London

Greece

Detroit

West Virginia

somewhere in Iowa—

somewhere in—

"Though the words were broken, yet she expressed herself in a won-
derful way."[27]

NOTES

1. Frank O'Hara, *Poems Retrieved* (San Francisco: City Lights Books, 2013),
11.

2. Frank O'Hara, *Lunch Poems* (San Francisco: City Lights Books, 1964), 19.

3. Kenneth Goldsmith, *Soliloquy* (New York: Granary Books, 2001), 338–39.

4. Kenneth Goldsmith, "Flarf is Dionysus. Conceptual Writing is Apollo."
Poetry (July/August 2009), 315.

5. Kenneth Goldsmith, *Uncreative Writing: Managing Language in the Digital
Age* (New York: Columbia Univ. Press, 2011), 83.

6. Bhanu Kapil, *Schizophrene* (New York: Nightboat Books, 2011), 51.

7. Bhanu Kapil, *Incubation: A Space for Monsters* (New York: Leon Works,
2006), 4.

8. *Schizophrene*, 46

9. *Incubation*, 43.

10. Bhanu Kapil, *Humanimal: A Project for Future Children* (Berkeley: Kelsey Street Press, 2009), 54.

11. *Schizophrene*, 71.

12. *Incubation*, 25.

13. *Humanimal*, 63.

14. *Schizophrene*, 15.

15. *Incubation*, 86.

16. *Schizophrene*, 52.

17. *Incubation*, 7.

18. *Humanimal*, 22.

19. *Incubation*, 10.

20. *Schizophrene*, i.

21. *Incubation*, 76.

22. *Humanimal*, 63-64.

23. *Schizophrene*, 53.

24. *Incubation*, 11.

25. *Schizophrene*, 61.

26. *Incubation*, 44.

27. *Humanimal*, 39.

language learning (4)
+ migration on
-mediations on
colonialism + identity

negotiate boundaries
identities
stereotypes
-challenge, exist,
make space,
question

NOTES TOWARD
AN AFTERWORD

WHAT ENTRAILS

MG ROBERTS

Dorothy Wang asks, is there an English and American poetics that accounts for this pathologized "I"—not the universal speaker but the unloved speaker? Is there a "you" that can meet this (anti-) narrative halfway? In this collection of critical essays, the pathologized "I" denotes an ongoing inquiry into the conditions of subjectivity concerning the shifting landscape of Asian American poetics of the last forty years. Reading these essays, I am drawn to the question, *what forces the feeling of an event*? In this case, I am speaking of an Asian American Woman's avant-garde poetics, a continuum, an occurrence of a process—much like the ionization of an atom—where tiny parts exist alone or in combination that constitute a whole.

> ... I was *Lai Oy*, to pull out of my pocket
> every day, after American school,
> even Saturday mornings,
> From *Nellie*, from *Where*, from *Which Place*
> to *Lai Oy*, to *Beautiful Love*.
>
> Between these names
> I never knew I would ever get lost.[1]

Through these essays, we negotiate the boundaries of the Asian American poem through the political and contextual identities of language and diaspora occurring over forty years to create an endocrine of subjectivity. What is the role of the "I" in an Asian American poetical landscape, where identity secretes and gender as an identity refuses stasis? What is a woman? In *The Vertical Interrogation of Strangers* Kapil writes:

> I don't know where to begin. But I know
>
> my elbow, my back tooth: throbbing
>
> I must.[2]

What does it mean to be an Asian American woman? What is an avant-garde Asian American Poetic? The loop occurs, arising from "analogous explorations of language and social location"—an index negotiating the boundaries of race and gender.[3] Its locus is seen in the works of Berssenbrugge, Wong, Kapil, and Kim, in gestural forms embodied by the gross movements of language to express meaning. How can I say this? I'm thinking of how sentences "are binding in terms of a system's great churning,"[4] of the ways in which phonemes create nervous system entanglement: a syntax for injury. "There's a circulation around her in incapillary space, empty or hollow, in relation to organs // . . . The form of her body is important, as how she is here, though there's no physical evidence of her physical suffering."[5]

A language emerges that celebrates and returns again and again to the invisible space of the pocket, its lint. The viscera of the pouch where the forgotten and discarded collect: immigrants, perceptions

93

of the body, motherhood, and the role of the "I" as a site; the mute language of things, abrasions whose duration of blips occur as memory/antimemory or narrative/antinarrative marking what has already occurred. As Yu writes in *Race and the Avant-Garde*, "A kind of echo, socially-grounded, collectively-produced and received in an era when such groundings are no longer possible—an attempt to create a community by aesthetic means."[6] An errata of gestures in which the whole of the past is there in the present, in protective shadow— branching mycelium fibers reaching to actualize itself in/through the animal/human body:

> At the edge of the jungle was a seam, a dense shedding of light green ribbons of bark. A place where things previously separate moved together in a wet pivot. I stood and walked towards it in a dream [...] Her elbow as thick as a knot. I said it was cartilage—the body incubating a curved space, an animal self.[7]

In reading these critical essays by Wang, Woo, Dowling, and Lee, I am reminded of the ways in which the phoneme and the lyric are actualized through the page—an event much like chewing the cud, a recurrent conversation. I am also reminded that I too—as an immigrant, a woman, a mother, and a poet of Asian American descent —am a part of this continuum of writers whose poetics have been "extracted from the maternal language, on the condition that the sounds of phonemes remain similar."[8]

> I want to have sex with what I want to become. This is a statement related to women arriving in a country it would be regressive to leave.[9]

An orange cliff holds the light, concave and convex from wind, as between alive and not alive, the boundary of a person touching you, as if the person were moisture leaving air, skin's respiration You hold her like pollen, like pollen in the air, gold and durable, more like a dry spring that continues holding sky.[10]

Voice

It catches its underside and drags it back
What sound do we make, "n", "h", "g"
Speak and it is sound in time[11]

Yes, the phoneme, the thing that returns to touch the surfaces of. The place where everything touches itself all at once—on the page.

NOTES

1. Nellie Wong, *Dreams in Harrison Railroad Park* (Berkeley: Kelsey Street Press, 1977), 9.

2. Bhanu Kapil, *The Vertical Interrogation of Strangers* (Berkeley: Kelsey Street Press, 2001), 11.

3. Timothy Yu, *Race and the Avant-Garde: Experimental and Asian American Poetry since 1965* (Stanford: Stanford Univ. Press, 2009), 163.

4. Amber DiPietra, "can experimental poetry provide a release/new pathway for those who have been 'sentenced,'" *fallinginrealtime* (blog), May 17, 2013, http://adipietra.blogspot.com/2013/05/can-experimental-poetry-provide.html

5. Mei-mei Berssenbrugge, *Endocrinology* (Berkeley: Kelsey Street Press), 1997, 2–4.

6. Timothy Yu, *Race and the Avant-Garde: Experimental and Asian American Poetry since 1965* (Stanford: Stanford Univ. Press, 2009), 6.

7. Bhanu Kapil, *Humanimal: A Project for Future Children* (Berkeley: Kelsey Street Press, 2009), 6.

8. Ibid., 29. Louis Wolfson as quoted by Bhanu Kapil.

9. Bhanu Kapil. *Incubation: A Space for Monsters* (New York: Leon Works, 2006), 4.

10. Mei-mei Berssenbrugge, *Four Year Old Girl* (Berkeley: Kelsey Street Press, 1998), 44.

11. Myung Mi Kim, *Under Flag* (Berkeley: Kelsey Street Press, 1991), 13.

CONTRIBUTORS

SARAH DOWLING is the author of three books of poetry, *DOWN* (Coach House, 2014), *Birds & Bees* (Troll Thread, 2012), and *Security Posture* (Snare, 2009). Her critical articles have appeared in *American Quarterly*, *Canadian Literature*, *GLQ*, *Journal of Medical Humanities*, and *Signs*. Sarah teaches at the University of Washington Bothell and is International Editor at *Jacket2*.

SUEYEUN JULIETTE LEE, a doctoral candidate in English from Temple University, edits Corollary Press, a chapbook series devoted to multiethnic innovate writing, and serves as a poetry editor for the Asian American Writers Workshop (AAWW) in New York City. A 2013 Pew Fellow of the arts, Juliette is the author of *That Gorgeous Feeling* (Coconut Books, 2008) and *Underground National* (Factory School Press, 2010). Her third collection, *Solar Maximum*, is forthcoming from Futurepoem Press in 2014. She currently teaches at the University of the Arts and Richard Stockton College of New Jersey.

MG ROBERTS teaches in the San Francisco Bay Area and is the author of the poetry collection *not so, sea* (Durga Press, 2014). Her work has appeared in the *Stanford Journal of Asian American Studies*, *Bombay Gin*, *Web Conjunctions*, *Shampoo*, and *How2*, among other publications.

DOROTHY WANG is the author of *Thinking Its Presence: Form, Race, and Subjectivity in Contemporary Asian American Poetry* (Stanford University Press, 2013). She teaches in the American Studies Program at Williams College.

MERLE WOO is a socialist feminist poet, author, activist, and retired lecturer in Women Studies, San Jose State and San Francisco State University. Fired twice from the University of California, Berkeley, Woo lodged free-speech lawsuits based on the violation of her First Amendment rights and discrimination on account of race, sex, sexuality and political ideology. She won reinstatement three times. She is the author of the poetry collection, *Yellow Woman Speaks: Selected Poems*, expanded and reissued by Radical Women Publications in 2003. In 1994, she received the humanitarian award from the Northern California Lesbian and Gay Historical Society.

TIMOTHY YU is Associate Professor of English and Asian American Studies and director of the Asian American Studies Program at the University of Wisconsin-Madison. He is the author of *Race and the Avant-Garde: Experimental and Asian American Poetry since 1965* (Stanford University Press). He is also the author of two poetry chapbooks, *15 Chinese Silences* (Tinfish, 2009) and *Journey to the West* (Barrow Street, 2006).

ACKNOWLEDGMENTS

Mei-mei Berssenbrugge, selected works from *Endocrinology* (1997), *Four Year Old Girl* (2011), *Sphericity* (1993), *Nest* (1998), published by Kelsey Street Press. Permission granted by author.

Bhanu Kapil, excerpts from *Incubation: A Space for Monsters* (New York: Leon Works, 2006). Reprinted by permission of Renee Gladman and Leon Works.

Bhanu Kapil, excerpts from *Schizophrene* (New York: Nightboat Books, 2011). Permission granted by Stephen Motika and Nightboat Books.

Bhanu Kapil, selected works from *The Vertical Interrogation of Strangers* (2001) and *Humanimal, a Project for Future Children* (2009), published by Kelsey Street Press. Permission granted by author.

Myung Mi Kim, selected work from *Under Flag* (Berkeley: Kelsey Street Press, 1998). Permission granted by author.

Myung Mi Kim, selections from "Thirty and Five Books," originally published in *Dura* (Los Angeles: Sun & Moon, 1999). *Dura* (10th anniversary edition) (Nightboat Books, 2008). Permission granted by Stephen Motika and Nightboat Books.

Myung Mi Kim, selected work from "Lamenta," originally published in *Commons* (Berkeley: Univ. of California Press, 2002). Permission granted by University of California Press.

Myung Mi Kim, selected work from *Penury* (Richmond, CA: Omnidawn Publishing, 2009). Reprinted by permission of Rusty Morrison.

Frank O'Hara, excerpt from "A Step Away from Them," originally published in *Lunch Poems* (San Francisco: City Lights Books, 1964). Reprinted by permission of Robert Sharrard and City Lights Books.

Frank O'Hara, excerpt, "Song (I'm going to New York!)" (1951), originally published in *Poems Retrieved* (Bolinas, CA: Grey Fox, 1970). Reprint by City Lights Books (San Francisco: City Lights Books, 2013). Permission granted by Robert Sharrard.

Juliana Spahr, excerpted work from her Preface to *Dura* (10th anniversary edition) (Nightboat Books, 2008). Permissions granted by author and Nightboat Books.

Nellie Wong, selected works from *Dreams in Harrison Railroad Park* (Berkeley: Kelsey Street Press, 1977). Permission granted by author.

Nellie Wong, selected work from *Breakfast Lunch Dinner* (San Francisco: Meridien PressWorks, 2012). Permission granted by author.

Nellie Wong, selected works from "Sisters Say No to War" and "Revolutionary Love," originally published in *HEArt (Human Equity through Art)*, 2002. Permission granted by author.

TIMOTHY YU

is Associate Professor of English and
Asian American Studies and Director of the
Asian American Studies Program at the University
of Wisconsin-Madison. He is the author of *Race and
the Avant-Garde: Experimental and Asian American
Poetry Since 1965* (Stanford University Press).
He is also the author of two poetry chapbooks,
15 Chinese Silences (Tinfish, 2009) and
Journey to the West (Barrow Street, 2006).